FINE CRAFTSMANSHIP IN WOOD

Fine Craftsmanship in Wood

Betty Norbury

Linden Publishing Co
Fresno, CA

Publisher's Note

The arrangement of the craftsmen included in this book is mainly alphabetical. Adjustments have been made where necessary to the making up and design processes at the editorial stage of production. A complete alphabetical list is included in the Index.

Photographic acknowledgements have been made within the text where known but where sources have not been identified we gratefully acknowledge the use of such material.

Library of Congress Cataloging-in-Publication Data
Norbury, Betty,
    Fine craftsmanship in wood / Betty Norbury.
        p.   cm.
    Includes index.
    ISBN 0–941936–18–X
    1. Wood-carving — Great Britain — Themes, motives.   2. Woodwork —
Great Britain — Themes, motives.   I. Title.
NK9743.N67   1990
674′.8–dc20
                                                            90–6336
                                                            CIP

Published August 1990 by
Linden Publishing Co, 3845 North Blackstone, Fresno, CA 93726, USA

Typeset in Palatino by Ann Buchan (Typesetters), Shepperton
Printed in Great Britain by BPCC Wheatons, Exeter

For my grandmother

Say not 'Good-night'; — but in some brighter clime
Bid me 'Good-morning'.

A.L. Barbauld

Introduction

It has been said, of furniture makers in particular, that "they don't make it like that any more" — this book proves beyond a shadow of a doubt that they do!

Perhaps it is a lack of knowledge of the contemporary scene that prompts this pessimistic remark. Craftsmen in the main are generally happy to work away quietly for their clients whose recommendations fill their order books, and only the initiated know and benefit from their existence.

Craftsmanship is as good as it ever was and, in some cases, with the use of new technology, better. Many of our contemporary designers have as much to offer as Chippendale or Sheraton did in their time. Designers whose work stands the test of time are not legion, perhaps a handful in the passage of a hundred years. We, in our generation, have our share of aspiring designers, some of whom will be listed with the likes of Mackintosh and Gimson in years to come. The same is true of our woodcarvers and sculptors, whose names will one day appear beside those of Riemenschneider, Gibbons and Barlach.

It is my intention in compiling this book to provide the reader with a picture of what is happening in the field of the designers and craftsmen in wood. Over the past three years, I have corresponded with some six hundred exponents of the various disciplines, attended their exhibitions, and avidly scoured the media for mention of them. From this broad view I have chosen a selection of around two hundred to represent what is on offer, as we go into the nineties, from the carefully and faithfully reproduced to the loudly, aggressively modern.

There have been no rigid rules and regulations as to who shall, and shall not, be included; it is not possible to mention every worker in wood, even if the publication were big enough. New workshops are constantly springing up and old established ones are being brought to my attention. Conversely, workshops close down or come to an end for any number of reasons.

All those included in the book work in small workshops, a few employ assistants, others work entirely alone, designing and making their work themselves. It is not unusual to find three or four craftsmen working together from the same address, but maintaining separate identities, or for them to form partnerships, complementing each other's abilities. It is generally a world of quiet, methodical working, unhurried by the pressures of the current expected lifestyle. And whilst an element of machinery is used, timber still has to be selected and matched, glue has to dry, and the majority of the work has to be hand finished.

Their training, ideas and ambitions are as diverse as their work. When asked to fill in a questionnaire for their inclusion in the book, some wrote comprehensively about the paths they envisage treading, the ideals that they worked to and the influences people, places and books have had on their chosen career. Others gave succinct potted histories, committing nothing of their inner selves to paper. There has been no attempt made to give a repeated set of historical facts with regard to training, age and achievements, allowing the reader, where possible, to glimpse the driving force behind this unique group of specialists.

The work illustrated has been chosen by the makers themselves, representing current work or classic pieces made in the past for which they still have a certain affection. I have, with difficulty, refrained from passing on my own opinions as to which I consider to be the best. I trust that within the brief I have worked to, the best are included. But I have my favourites, as do we all. Personal likes and dislikes as far as designs are concerned are subjective, and I would like to think I have been impartial, allowing the readers of this book to decide what they do or do not enjoy. Like it or hate it — it's part of today.

The opportunities to see work such as that illustrated in this book are all too few. Exhibition facilities for makers are difficult and costly to come by. It is not, therefore, generally known how easy it is to buy a piece of work made in a small workshop, or how diverse are the styles and the costs involved. That people should give equal credence, if not preference, to an individually made piece of furniture as to that from a furniture shop or an antique dealer is one of my driving ambitions. And that a wood sculpture should receive equal merit with a bronze; the wood sculpture can never be repeated, the bronze can and often is.

For craftsmen to be able to sell their work or accept commissions we have to know that they exist. Many now leaving college, or having already passed through some aspect of industry or retailing are very aware of the need for marketing skills to complement those of designing and making, but many are not able to maintain the constant pursuit of sales, commissions, exhibition opportunities and necessary public profiles to make a financial success of their work. This is frequently the cause of their demise.

Through this book I would like to make many more people aware of the opportunities to own items made especially for them; pieces made by artists and craftsmen which will capture the imagination and bring both them and the maker an invisible but unbreakable tie of pleasure and shared aesthetic experience.

Betty Norbury

Andrew Alcock

The influence of the late 19th century is evident in the piece illustrated here by Andrew Alcock, who has worked with wood for the past twenty years, the last ten of which he has spent as a professional furniture maker. Andrew has recently become the director of the family upholstery business, H.G. Lomas, but he will continue to make individual pieces to commission as time allows, putting the partnership of cabinetmaking and upholstery to good use.

Victorian style lady's spoonback chair in mahogany. Frame, Andrew Alcock; upholstery, H.G. Lomas.

Photograph courtesy of Studio Five.

Peter Bailey

Peter Bailey's approach to furniture designing and making has been influenced by a career in architecture where fitness for purpose in the product has to be achieved through the constraints of the building process. Peter has now been working with wood since 1982 and works mainly in native hardwoods.

Captain's chair. Oak with laminations of walnut incorporated into the back and arms. The seat is slatted and fitted with a hide cover.

Photograph courtesy of Ian Southern.

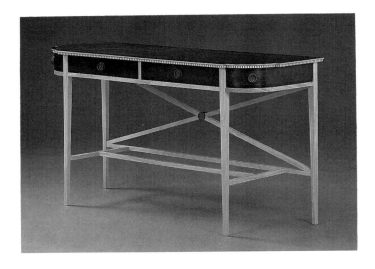

Console table of sycamore and ebony.

Architectural desk in satinwood with bronze fittings.

Detail of dining table top in ash, sycamore, ebony and satinwood.

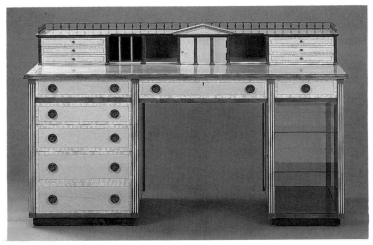

Nick Allen

Nick Allen's furniture has a distinct personal style influenced by the late 18th and 19th century and Palladian architecture. He combines traditional construction and decorative techniques with strong designs and colours. Extensive research has resulted in the use of different species of wood for veneers and staining. He uses exotic timber, incorporating intricate inlay; and natural and stained veneer finishes, combined with bronze and other handmade fittings.

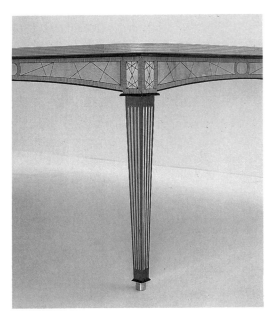

John Ambrose

Forty years ago John Ambrose served his apprenticeship as a joiner and cabinetmaker, and has been working with wood ever since. Essentially a woodturner, he would like to develop his own style of turned sculpture, but for the moment he is working on reviving the old method of producing sets, or nests of bowls from one blank. This will be particularly beneficial when using expensive, beautifully grained timber, bearing in mind the considerable waste factor incurred with conventional turning methods.

Set of three ladles in yew.

John Anderson

John Anderson's mirrors and boxes reflect personal interests and enthusiasms: ships and the sea, forests, birds, hidden gardens. Painted doors and trompe l'oeil windows open to reveal secret mirrors and other worlds. He values this element of mystery and surprise and will continue to delight his clients with pieces that are always more than meets the eye on first acquaintance.

Boat box.

Freddie Baier

Having worked with wood since he was "knee high to a grasshopper", Freddie Baier has become in his own words "... a very committed worker, permanently interested in pushing the envelope of the field of furniture on all fronts: subjective, objective, procedural, conceptual, futuristic, etc. My greatest knowledge and ability is in wood, therefore wood is the major component usually. The majority of my income comes from making "one of a kind" commissions. Included in each project is a demand that some positive headway is achieved in pushing that all encompassing envelope."

Restored and rebuilt piano — finished in black with blue opalescent lacquer by Page Lacquer Company.

Photograph courtesy of Philip Grey.

Tray stand in sycamore — pop rivets are used to hold the undulating curves of the support.

"Sardines", lime.

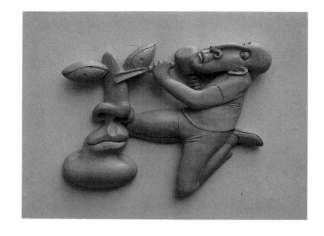

"Chiselled features", lime.

John Baldwin

In a continuing attempt to surprise himself and hold a dialogue with the viewers of his work, John Baldwin chooses to carve wood rather than express himself in words. Trained in sculpture at the Camberwell School of Art, he has worked in modern materials such as polystyrene and fibreglass, making such diverse pieces as replacement chimney pots and domes for conservation, elephant slides for childrens' play areas and more finely worked decorative coats of arms. Seven years ago at the age of 42, John gave up the security of paid employment for the uncertainty of life as a woodsculptor, although he still does a little freelance work for his previous firm. His first wooden piece was a sculptural jigsaw puzzle, and he enjoyed this concept so much that he made a series of them as small batch runs. His more individual work is sold through galleries and at group exhibitions.

"Beneath the sheets", lime.

David Bailey

David Bailey started his career in wood as a turner, but felt that he would like to make something a little more taxing. After his redundancy he began experimenting with furniture design, but it was the fine furniture course at Buckinghamshire College which was to give direction to his ideas, in particular a visit to the collection of Arts and Crafts furniture held by the Cheltenham Museum. He especially liked the attention to fine details and selection of materials, but most of all he liked the feeling of quality evoked by the backs of cabinets finished to the same degree of craftsmanship as the fronts. Now David is daring to tread in the footsteps of the exponents of the Arts and Crafts Movement as can be seen in his writing desk. It is a piece of a matching range of furniture which he feels offers simple yet distinctive design qualities, and demonstrates a meticulous attention to detail.

Writing desk and chair in American white oak.
Detail of writing desk and chair (right).

Chris Barney

Having built boats and designed bridges, Chris Barney's main ambition now is ". . . to produce furniture which, while unequivocally of the present, will be respected in the future. Most of what I do is in English hardwoods, left as naturally as is practicable, and one of my greatest pleasures is to see people feeling the work — often running their hands over it without seeming to realise what they are doing."

Desk in English cherry and walnut with leather writing surface. The side trays pivot on a brass bar, allowing them to swing forward.

Robert Beal

Robert Beal uses the ideals of 18th century craftsmen as a standard for his own work, making contemporary furniture with the same care and attention to detail as his predecessors. Robert strives ''. . . to continue designing and producing new and exciting pieces of furniture that will be a never-ending delight to live with, raising people's spirits rather than flattening them.'

Chairs and sideboard in maple.

Hugh Birkett

Living and working from the delightful Cotswold village of Moreton in the Marsh, Hugh Birkett has been designing and making furniture for the last 40 years. Gimson and the Barnsleys have been a considerable influence in his work, but this is hardly surprising when one considers that he was a pupil of Oliver Morel, one of Edward Barnsley's students.

Elliptical display cabinet in Cuban mahogany.

16

Richard Blizzard

Richard Blizzard describes himself as a catalyst, an inspiration to the toy and model makers. Almost twenty years ago Richard began to make wooden toys for his son; this developed from a hobby, whilst teaching at primary school, to a more than full time occupation. His articles in the trade press struck just the right note with other enthusiasts, and now his television programmes and books take up eleven months of the year, leaving him very little time for making for himself. All the prototypes that he makes for the B.B.C. are given to childrens' homes and hospitals. The most famous of these was the model of the Rolls Royce Silver Ghost and the company made two hundred and fifty minature Rolls Royce radiators especially for the wood replicas. Richard is responsible for bringing much pleasure not only to the makers of his designs, but to the many children who receive them as gifts. His motto is from the poet Robert Bridges: "I too will something make And joy in the making."

Model of the Rolls Royce Silver Ghost.

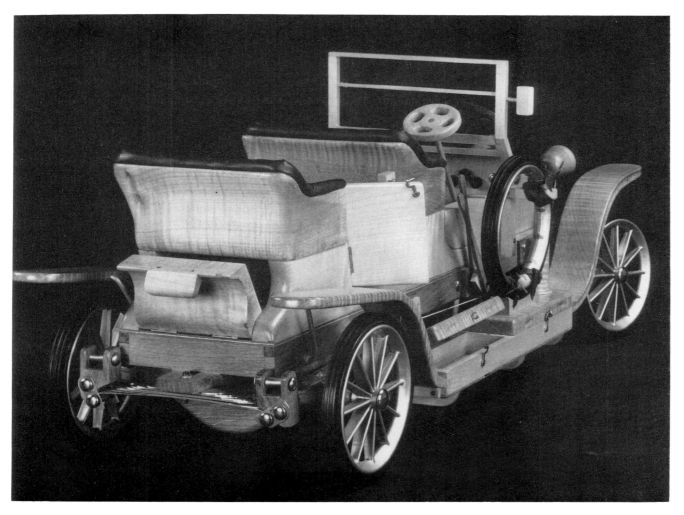

17

David Bowerman

"When I create a piece of furniture for a client I am aiming for perfection in design, as I perceive it, within the parameters of their brief and also perfection in the execution of the piece. It is a touchstone rarely, if ever, achieved but gives me something to aim for."
David Bowerman.

Writing desk in acacia, cedar of Lebanon and mahogany.

Detail of above showing open drawer with removable wooden pots and divisions for writing paper.

Kenneth Bowers

Even after 40 years, craftsman Kenneth Bowers feels he has never retired from his apprenticeship as he is continually learning, creating with both mind and hands. His world is one of an idyllic existence . . . one he does not wish to change.

Box in English walnut.

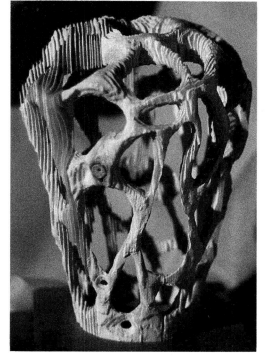

Christopher Briggs

For several years Christopher Briggs has been using the technique of abrasive blasting to produce varying effects. The blasting removes the soft part of the wood and leaves the lines of grain outstanding. Depth of cut can also be varied from actually piercing the wood to just texturing the surface.

"Migraine" in softwood.

Jean Burhouse

Whilst studying cabinetmaking at Kirkcaldy College of Technology Jean Burhouse received the accolade of top student of the year. In 1984 she set up her own workshop in Inver working only to commission. Her singleminded attention to her customers' requirements has ensured a full order book.

Lady's writing desk in pommelle mahogany.

Jeremy Broun

"In a nutshell, my only concern with the past is to use *tradition* as a catalyst to express the energy and *life* of woodworking today and therefore hope my work reflects the age I live in, which I personally believe is a Golden Age of Craftsmanship." Jeremy Broun.

Caterpillar rocking chair in grey stained birch plywood with red lacquered mahogany slats.

Fraser Budd

Fraser Budd is continually motivated by the excellent standard of work of other designer/makers. He is fascinated by proportion, balance and geometry as well as the use of lines, both straight and curved, to produce designs. His own work is uninhibited by the constraints of the power equipment in the workshop as he enjoys employing hand techniques and tries to ignore the consideration of how a piece will be constructed and made until the overall form and style has been decided. At present Fraser is developing a range of pieces all based around the same design theme, and his future plans include producing more designs that are recognisably his own. As Head of Craft, Design and Technology at a large comprehensive school in Bristol he is well placed to achieve his other ambition which is to pass on his knowledge both by writing and by teaching practical skills.

Blanket/storage chest in figured sycamore with rosewood banding and black inlay.

Embroiderer's compendium chest in figured sycamore with rosewood banding and black inlay. After lifting the lid, the front panel folds down and slides away revealing five drawers; The lid contains the fold down compartment.

Anthony Bryant

Anthony Bryant discovered woodturning at the age of thirteen and it became a time consuming hobby even during the years that he worked in commerce. Following several short residential courses with Mike Law, an industrial woodturner, he resigned from safe paid employment in 1982 to become a vessel maker. Since then he has been single minded in his attempt to make a success of his chosen career, sacrificing many things along the way, using a combination of hard work, positive attitude, direction of purpose and luck to ensure that he need not compromise his work in pursuit of money. Achieving this position has not encouraged him to rest on his laurels, but to set two new goals: firstly to make the perfect bowl, and secondly to move more into pure sculpture, leaving behind the machine which inevitably restricts his work. Wood will be Anthony's medium for a long time to come; he does not feel attracted to ceramics or clay in the same way. His work can be seen at the many exhibitions he takes part in, or at craft and art galleries up and down the country.

Group of spalted beech vessels (below).

Burr oak vessels (right).

Matthew Burt

Matthew Burt's fascination with the fabrication of objects is evident here in his unorthodox ruminative chair, commissioned by Southern Arts and designed to their brief — "A chair that is witty and speaks of its intent." The chair is to be awarded to the person showing the most initiative in marketing the Arts, and is made in three elms. The back and worry globes in burr elm, the arms and legs in wych elm and the main cross rails in English elm. The ropes, an allusion to the Indian rope trick, are laminated and carved sycamore. More conformist, but with the structure still very much in evidence is his hall table, made of ripple sycamore with bird's-eye maple top. Matthew did his formal training as a furniture maker and designer at Rycotewood College back in the '70's followed by a two year apprenticeship and has been working for himself for the last twelve years.

Ruminative chair.

Photograph courtesy of David Wiltshire.

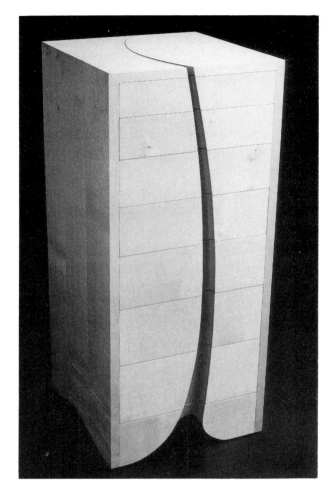

Chest of drawers in American black walnut.

Sycamore chest of drawers, with a pink lacquered line which cuts into the front to form handles, and runs on over the top.

Ashley Cartwright

Not content with a first class honours diploma in art and design, Ashley Cartwright went on to obtain an M.A. at the Royal College of Art in 1973. It was here that he met David Pye and joined the ranks of the many craftsmen influenced by Pye's teaching. He also found the three years that he worked with John Makepeace both helpful and encouraging. After this extensive preparatory experience Ashley began working for himself and has been doing so ever since, allowing time out to teach at Loughborough College of Art and Design. Travelling around the world has played an important inspirational role in his work and further journeys to other countries, experiencing the culture and way of life, is seen as an important part of his future development as a designer, rather than maker of furniture.

Cerdan

Twenty-three years ago, when Geoff Godschalk had finished his four year diploma course in furniture production and design at the London College of Furniture, there was not the same opportunity for one to work alone from a small workshop. The first fourteen years of his career were, therefore, spent in the furniture industry, initially in middle management, and later as a production consultant. He has retained his links with the industry and continues his consultancy work on a freelance basis. In 1980 he started out on his own and he enjoys working for both private and corporate clients as well as making prototypes for the furniture industry. Some of his designs are suitable for limited batch production and are sold through retail outlets, among them is the Cerdan chair.

The Cerdan Chair. Laminated pear and leather upholstery.

Dining table in American cherry; seats ten in comfort. The centre is loose to allow for movement and held in place with toggles. The matching chairs have free floating backs shaped to the natural curve of the spine.

Paul Caton

"I have been influenced by the great
sculptors of both the past and present as
well as by craftsmen working in a variety
of new mediums. To me, the actual
physical, mental and spiritual involvement
of the work is a form of Zen, which
hopefully is conveyed to the eventual
owner of the sculpture. The work is meant
to be visual, tactile, functional and
ultimately meditative." Paul Caton.

Bowls in yew.

Chameleon

"One main feature of my work
is ease of production. I try to
rationalise everything down to
the most economic and yet
satisfactory form of
manufacture. This gives my
work, as a whole, a common
theme of simplicity in its
design." Andrew Woodcock.

*The Wassenaar suite. The black lacquered
frame is constructed of maple. The jointing
method is basically the same throughout,
using a cross half lap. The arms and back are
of English ash and slats support the seat. Fat,
chunky leather cushions contrast with the
rigidity of the frame.*

26

Samuel Chan

Samuel Chan spent seven years at college gaining a diploma in furniture studies and a Master of Arts degree in furniture design. Working in London, he now makes furniture in naturally finished timbers which he feels is of simple design, with an emphasis on detail. The design for the *Lamination Chair* evolved from a Chinese character meaning simply, "girl". The object of the design is to use curves of one radius, making it easy to manufacture as only one former is needed. It is constructed of beech veneers. The roots of the design for the side table also spring from the Far East. Made from English oak, it is the realisation and expression of the Oriental influence on Samuel's work.

Side table in English oak.
Lamination Chair constructed of beech veneers.

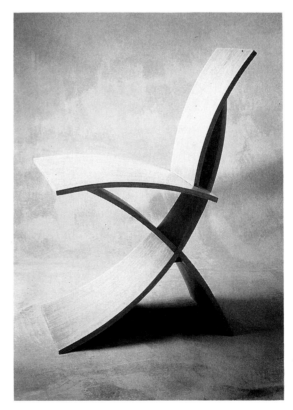

Detail of maker's symbol.

Philip Chambers

Philip Chambers is director of the musical instruments repair course at Merton College, Morden in Surrey. In his spare time he is a guitar maker carrying out the work from his home workshop in Sutton. His guitars have been singled out for exhibitions and awarded gold medals as well as being chosen for a demonstration at a lecture by guitar player José Romanillas. Philip's aim has been to make individual custom-made guitars for musicians.

Classical guitar with spruce soundboard, bird's-eye maple back and ribs, tulipwood bandings, Brazilian rosewood bridge, ebony fingerboard and Macassar ebony veneered peg head.
12 string, steel strung acoustic guitar. Spruce soundboard; Brazilian rosewood back; mahogany neck with ebony bridge and fingerboard. Inlays used include ebony, holly, abalone, 9ct gold and mother-of-pearl.

Jess Christman

Forty minutes outside Edinburgh, at the edge of the Lammermuir Hills is where Jess Christman has chosen to set up his home and workshop. From here he fulfils commissions for interior fittings as well as individual pieces of furniture. Home grown timber is used for the majority of his work, being felled and converted under his own watchful eye.

Cabinet in ripple sycamore, ash, oak, walnut and maple.

Neil Clarke

"I set out to design and make contemporary domestic furniture in the Arts and Crafts tradition from solid English hardwoods, featuring traditional jointing techniques and contrasting timber colours. Emphasis is placed upon clean, contemporary lines, making the most of the natural wood grain in conjunction with fine detailing such as bevels and chamfers, to catch the interplay of light and shade."

Neil Clarke

Jewellery chest with mirror in olive ash and lacewood.

29

Brian Cohen

Brian Cohen is a restorer and maker of stringed musical instruments. His work is sold to musicians, ranging from serious students at college to top professional players at home and abroad. His restoration work is sought by private collectors and major dealers.

The great masters, whose instruments have become the "benchmark" by which all players assess others, have been a source of inspiration to him, and he has studied their methods extensively and incorporates them in his own work as often as is feasible. He uses them as a springboard rather than copying them, striving to create his own style, but feeling, inevitably, that it is influenced by everything he sees and absorbs.

Whilst most of his work is original, he prefers to call some of his work "reconstructions" based on the originals, either of the Baroque, Italian or Spanish style. Making instruments has been a way of life for him for sixteen years. In the past he has made a variety of stringed instruments, from early guitars to lutes and viola de gamba. He acknowledges that perhaps his interests are too broad, and says he intends to limit himself to the classical guitar and the cello. However, as an instrument maker, he knows he will not be able to resist the occasional excursions into other fields which are greatly tempting.

Brian Cohen works to the highest technical level, giving today's demanding players what they need — good playing instruments, well made, hand-made.

Detail of scroll and pegbox; pegs in boxwood.

Cello made in maple, based on Goffriller, circa 1690. Length of back 28 7/8". All fittings are boxwood. Table in spruce.

30

10 course lute, scale length 63 cm, top made from spruce, ribs in maple with neck
and pegbox veneered in ebony and snakewood, tuning pegs in cocobolo.

8 course lute, scale length 67 cm, top made from spruce, ribs from yew,
with the neck veneered in holly and ebony, turning pegs in cocobolo.

Classical guitar, scale length 65
cm, top made from spruce, with
the back and sides in Brazilian
rosewood, cedar neck.

Max Cooper

Max Cooper served a four year apprenticeship with Bernard Jack, a local antique furniture restorer and cabinet maker, and was then taught marquetry cutting and all other aspects of veneer work by Andrew Oliver at periodic intervals through the next five years. He also took further courses in restoration, polishing and woodcarving at the CoSira workshops in London. Following this intensive period of training Max set up his own workshop for fifteen years in the garden of his parents' home. As his workload and reputation increased he outgrew these premises and moved to renovated farm buildings with two assistants. Whilst he still undertakes specialized restoration, most of his time is spent making new marquetry pieces for his clients.

This marquetry chair, in Santos rosewood, is one of a pair made for an overseas client.

Walnut marquetry longcase clock.

Detail of longcase clock.

Marquetry collector's box in East Indian satinwood with six rosewood bowfronted drawers.

Photographs courtesy of Tony Boydon.

33

Twin playing card box in dyed veneer and ivory
lined with fiddle-back sycamore.

Box in blue and white quilted maple.
After "Harlequin" by Picasso.

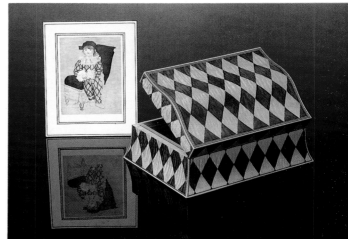

Curved-form harlequin design tea caddy in
dyed veneers with two fitted internal tea boxes
in burr oak and a fitted glass blending bowl,
lined with figured beech throughout.

Andrew Crawford

Making fine decorative boxes is only one of Andrew Crawford's occupations; he also teaches music, enjoying the flexibility and compatibility of the two disciplines. The first box he ever made was a twenty-first birthday present for a girlfriend and though he swore it had taken so long he would never repeat the experience, he was hooked.

He began sharing workshop space with a friend who was employed in antique restoration. Initially, Andrew restored and repaired musical instruments, for which he had been trained at the London College of Furniture, while he developed his boxes. The basic "flared" shape that he uses for the sides of many of his pieces is derived from the very solid look that trees have at their base.

In an attempt to use less traditional material, he is successfully experimenting with dyed veneers. One project he is working on at the moment is to echo the highly coloured costume designs in some 18th century works of art, particularly the harlequin pattern commonly worn by members of the Commedia dell'arte troupes of the period. He is also working on his own versions of some standard Victorian boxes, tea caddies, writing slopes and sewing boxes, incorporating the work of other craftsmen wherever feasible — for example a ceramic mixing bowl for the tea caddy and perhaps a miniature tapestry for the work box.

Jewellery box in bird's-eye maple.

Jewellery casket in book-matched burr walnut.

35

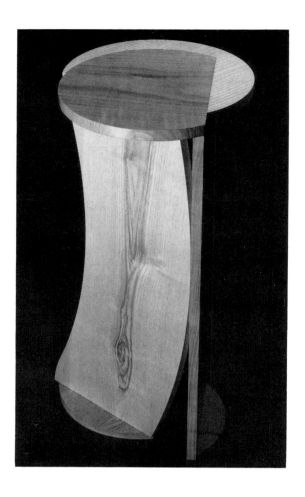

Benedict Critchley

Benedict Critchley's formal qualifications include a Bachelor of Arts [honours degree] in art history from Trinity College, Cambridge, and an advanced chair and cabinet making course at Shrewsbury College. He has been working on his own since 1986 and is currently developing this occasional table-cum-stool as a batch production item. He has found that it is proving a great challenge to preserve the object's sculptural impact through the constraints of making it efficiently.

Jeremy Cornwell

Jeremy Cornwell is fascinated by monumental architecture and design, whether it is Nature's work or man-made. The Giant's Causeway in Northern Ireland and the Pyramids are just two of the landmarks from which he draws his inspiration. His furniture is designed and built to have the same primal quality.

Occasional table/stool in solid elm and ash with ash veneer.

Bench made in ash.

Side table made in Baltic granite, black walnut and sycamore.

Stephen Cooper

Stephen Cooper is a completely self-taught worker in wood. Having been told at an early age that a career in wood would lead to a dead end, he trained as a design engineer, an occupation which he followed for over a decade, making victorian toys and turned wooden ware in his free time. A spinning wheel commissioned by his sister was Stephen's turning point. The piece won an award in London in 1983, and fired with new enthusiasm, he set out to begin working for himself. For six years he has been making more traditional furniture, spinning wheels and treen. His workshop is situated at the rear of an antique shop/gallery in Tring, through which he sells some of his work.

A table top or lover's spinning wheel in Indian rosewood with mother-of-pearl inlay and elk horn finials.

Scandinavian-style spinning wheel in padauk with ivory finials.

Cumberlidge & Jenkinson

"Five years ago Helen Cumberlidge peered into the gloom of my Dartmouth workshop in search of a particular piece of wood, at the same time declaring her intention to train as a furniture restorer. I grandly ignored this ambition of hers and began to teach and encourage her in the skills of woodcarving. We now work together from our workshop at Dartington.

It can be argued that to survive efficiently man needed the basic tools with which to bore holes and with which to shape materials, and also something to hold food and water. It is overly simplistic, I know, but we derive a great deal of pleasure in the fact that our developing collection of sculptured vessels depends, at least initially, on these basic echoes.

It is of paramount importance that our work be as flawless as possible in its execution, and, as we have discovered, total planning is essential. I have always admired well conceived, robust, textured sculpture but there is special satisfaction in aiming for a certain fine resonance in the finished piece. With every stroke, the tip of the cutting edge must carry with it the focus of the carver's mind and desire, and also a tiny distillation of the finished whole.

The wood is incredibly valuable to us. Most of the pieces used come from trees that have taken perhaps three of my lifetimes and more to grow. Consequently, shelves in the studio are full of potted seedlings — walnut, ash, laburnum and maple. Put it down to sentimentality if you wish, but it is an exercise in putting back some of that which has been taken out. Every worker of wood should grow a few trees." Roderick Jenkinson

"Germination" one of a series in plum

''August 31st 1986'' in walnut

''Bohm's Hypothesis'' in walnut

''Dancing Vase'' in laurel

''Untitled'' composite timber substitute

''Maple Leaves'' in sycamore

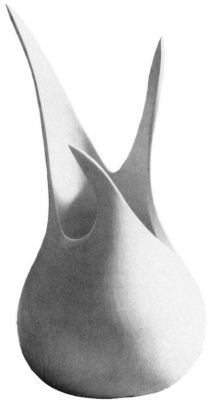

39

Chris Dunseath

"My sculpture over the last few years has been concerned with the human form. *Limewood Figure* continues my interest in direct carving and employs diverse cultural and historical references. These influences have ranged from the work of 17th century German woodcarvers to Grinling Gibbons and from early Egyptian sculpture to Indian temple carvings. My sculptures can take over a year to make and this gradual carving process generates very close observation and enables considerable attention to be paid to every slight modification of shape and form. *Limewood Figure* was intended to convey a sense of powerful stillness and contemplative calm." Chris Dunseath

"Limewood Figure", the base of which, when viewed from a distance produces the perceptual illusion of alternating faces or pedestal.

Eric Cooper

With a background of a full and varied artistic education, culminating at the Royal College of Art, Eric Cooper has been working with wood for the past forty years, the last eighteen of which he has worked professionally as a furniture maker and restorer as well as in other aspects of woodcraft. His letter heading describes him intriguingly as Eric J. Cooper, Artist, Craftsman and General Surgeon.

Carved commemorative platter in cherry.

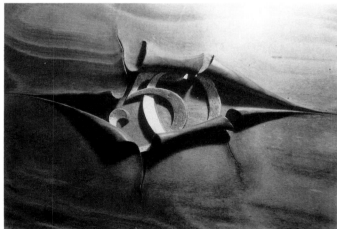

Roger Curry

"Within my furniture I hope to achieve a visual and structural unity, and that each piece has something of me. Some of my work is quite aesthetically sculptural but as a furniture designer and craftsman it has always been my main aim to make pieces that are physically functional."

Wine table in fiddle-back sycamore.

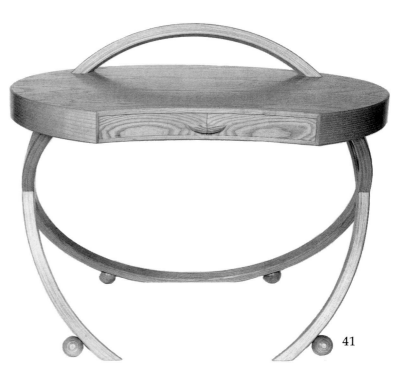

Chair in ash with leather seat and back rest. Blue leather.

Writing desk, ash.

Photographs courtesy of Peter Bartlett.

41

Detail

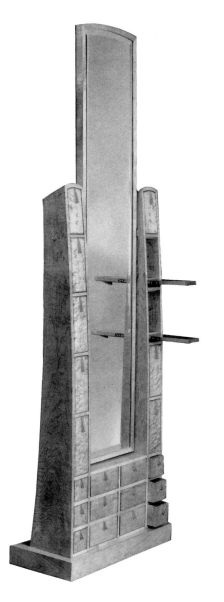

After studying furniture design at Middlesex Polytechnic Andy Jackson opened his own company Design Works in 1984. Five years later when Gordon Russell graduated from his fine craft and furniture course at Buckinghamshire College, they formed a partnership called Detail, designing and making individual pieces of furniture and small production runs. Fairs and exhibitions are favourite selling venues for them, their work attracting buyers from around the world, the most memorable to date being an American client who ordered a dozen chairs at a Paris show for his New York shop.

"I am particularly interested by mass-market art deco product design — a kind of bastardisation of cubism, modernism and neo-classicism; and furniture in the Beidermier style — more refined, but often just as irreverent in its reference to classicism. I enjoy random and often humorous plundering of these past styles, to create forms that are still exciting and very much current." Andy Jackson

Reflection of a Hoarder, bird's-eye maple with cherry detail. Designed and made by Gordon Russell.

Sofa in bird's-eye maple with ebony inlays, patinated copper inlays and specially cast bronze motifs inlaid along the back rail. Traditionally upholstered in a watermarked damask fabric. Designed and made by Andy Jackson.

Photographs courtesy of Lucinda Symons.

Desk and matching chair in European oak with black detailing, fluted columns and chevron veneer work with grey leather panel.

Oak dining table.

Philip Dobbins

Although he had neither a conventional apprenticeship, nor an "Art School" start, Philip Dobbins has been producing fine furniture for about ten years. He works alone and necessarily avoids work which involves extensive fitting on site. Individual pieces are not, however, limited to size, and a sixteen foot boardroom table is his largest piece to date. Commissions are fairly evenly split between period copies and his own contemporary designs.

This oak desk and chair were designed for a large insurance company, the "deco" styling complementing the existing office interior. The dining table develops the theme using ebony and ivory; the dining chairs are on the drawing board.

Brian Dollemore

"My craft is the portrayal in miniature of the shapes and textures of British traditional building, carved and engraved in solid timbers selected to accentuate form and suggest colour. Occasional excursions into polite architecture are provided by clients whose homes are more formal but, whatever the building, I am striving for disciplined scale and line, yet with the liveliness of positive toolwork. . . No-one, it seems, has specialised this way before — the problems and solutions are of my own making and some of my techniques are, therefore, probably unique."
Brian Dollemore

Barn at Monks Eleigh, Suffolk, in elm. Scale 1/16" = 1'. (length 2½").
House at Longparish, Hampshire, in elm. Scale 1/8" = 1'. (length 5½").

House near Dorking, Surrey, in light walnut on an ebonised oak plinth. Scale 1/8" = 1'. (length 12½"). By kind permission of the clients.

44

Resurrection figure for St Ovens Manor Chapel in Jersey.

A pair of relief panels, carved in lime, from a set of stations of the cross from Kirkwall Roman Catholic Church.

Marvin Elliott

"My work is my occupation, my hobby, my relaxation, and part of my excitement. It is 95% of my waking life. My only desire is to do the best I can, with as much passion as I can get for the work and subject matter. The problem with commissioned works is that some light the light, others only glimmer.

My influences have been most of the classic sulptors in wood, stone and bronze. I collect churches like others collect stamps, and have photographs and postcards of most of the church carvings throughout Germany and France and I am now concentrating on Spain and Portugal. I admire the church for their past patronage of many disciplines of the arts.

The future is confusing. The older I get the less time there is to produce all of my ideas. There may not be enough time so, as I get older we may see a deterioration in standards in order that I can achieve more and more.

I vote Green and plant a tree every three months to make up for what I've taken." Marvin Elliott

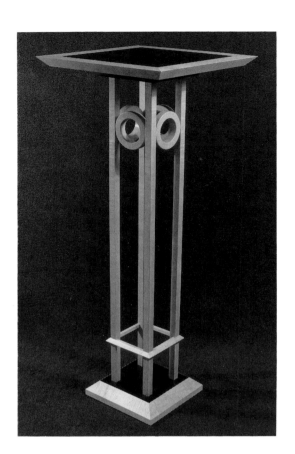

Stephen Down

Stephen Down works from Shelly Farm Workshop in the heart of rural Northumberland, and it is the landscape of this beautiful county that initially influenced his furniture design. Over the past ten years that he has been making furniture his objective has been "... to develop forms that re-examine traditional views without rejecting traditional construction techniques."

Plant/display stand in sycamore with Macassar ebony veneer.

Frank Egerton

Frank Egerton's desire to draw and make has been with him since he was a child, even whilst teaching and raising a young family, he would find a little spare time to pursue his ideas and develop his woodworking skills. At the age of 33 he and his wife Bridget began to work together full time making "toys". Fourteen years on, Frank continues to delight us with his work which he wants "... to reach as large an audience as possible through creating fantasy, which has no particular purpose other than to make people smile."

Noah's Ark.

46

Robert Ellwood

Robert Ellwood designs and makes furniture in a wide range of styles and media, as diverse a range, in fact, as the clients for whom he works. Many of his pieces rely on traditional native timbers and construction, often combining timber with slate, marble or metals, and he sees his work becoming increasingly sculptural and delicate, with the more frequent inclusion of colour and decoration. He finds it important, although not essential, to have a readily identifiable client for his work — to design for someone rather than for something. He has been profoundly influenced by working as a young man with Edward Barnsley and subsequently studying the work of others in this important genre: William Morris, Ernest Gimson, Charles Rennie Mackintosh, Joseph Hoffman and Frank Lloyd-Wright.

Puzzle in Indian rosewood and silver, based on the Ridings of Yorkshire. This sculpture consists of a number of cubes that fit into a grid. The vertical dimensions have been exaggerated to emphasise the hills, dales and coastline of Yorkshire.

Rocking chair in English ash. This organic piece results from some early experimental work in steaming and laminating. The chair is structurally sound and derives just the right degree of flexibility from the construction and materials used.

47

Alan Englefield

When he left Rycotewood College, Alan Englefield set up his
workshop near Salisbury with his wife Claire and they have
worked together for eight years now, selling their work to
private clients. His ambition is to encourage public awareness
of the growing choice of high quality, hand-made furniture
being produced by individual small workshops, and to play a
constructive part in the current revival of British cabinetmaking.

Ladder back chair in sycamore and apple.
Sewing box in sycamore with suede lining.
Photographs courtesy of Graham Photography

Side table in sycamore and burr elm with English walnut cross banding.

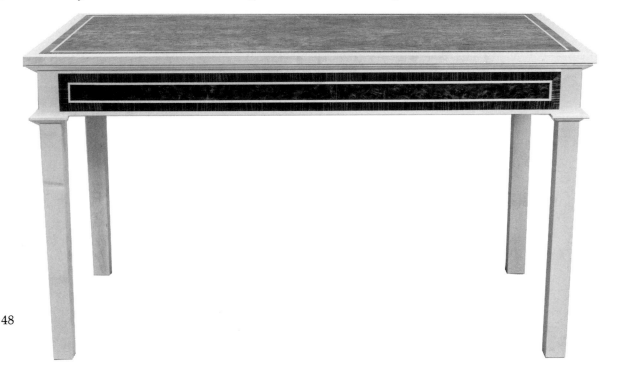

Sean Feeney

Sean Feeney's ambition is modest, it is to achieve a reasonable standard of living from designing and making furniture, and that his clientele should continue to grow. This desk and chair, made from Macassar ebony and sycamore is a less modest testament to Sean's ability.

He works at his Warwickshire based workshop with his brother Michael, and two assistants. Commissioned work is the mainstay of the business, their clients coming to them mainly by recommendation, along with occasional contract work for other designers. Sean Feeney Furniture was founded ten years ago, after Sean had spent two years at Rycotewood College, and eighteen months as a pattern maker and a short spell as an antique restorer.

Desk and chair in Macassar ebony and sycamore.

49

Nicholas Dyson

Nicholas Dyson studied English at Cambridge University, lived in Scandinavia, and worked as an academic publisher's editor in London, before deciding to become a furniture maker. He spent a year at Parnham House, followed by a brief period in the London workshops of David Field and Martin Grierson, after which he shared a workshop on the Somerset/Dorset border. He settled in Oxfordshire in 1984.

Working with a small team of four accomplished craftsmen, most of his work is made in response to specific commissions. Some from private clients wanting pieces for their homes to increasingly more enquiries from companies and institutions through architectural and design practices. Very few pieces are made speculatively for sale or exhibition. The work is unsigned, as Nicholas reacts slightly against the over-personalisation of work, believing that if it is of any worth or interest there will inevitably be a record of who designed and made it. He sees personal achievement as a moving target '. . . At different times one is trying to achieve different things. Different horizons according to how high one is lifting one's head at the time. But thinking more generally — to increase the number of good things in the world; to provide a satisfying set of working possibilities for one's colleagues; and to satisfy the private demon that asks, what have you left in the world?' "

Triple fronted glazed bookcase in sycamore and American black walnut.

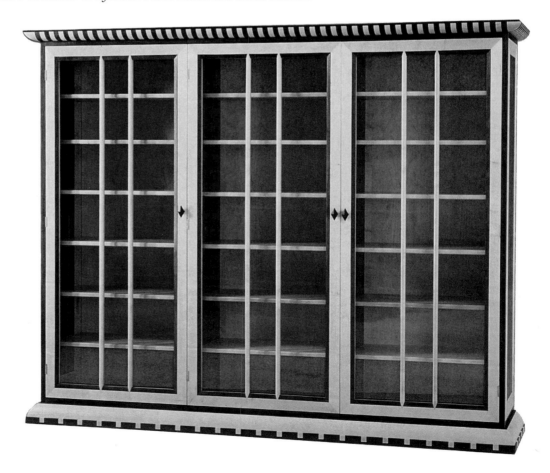

Two drawer writing table in European cherry.

Dining table and chairs (centre) to seat ten in solid sycamore and American black walnut.

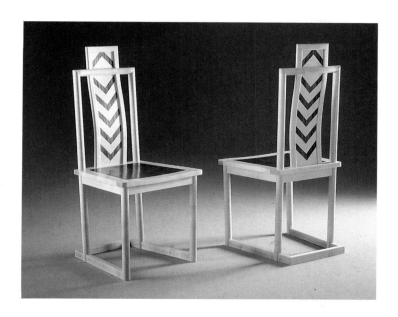

Semi-elliptical console table in maple, pear and rosewood.

Winged credenza in ripple ash veneer and solid Indian rosewood.

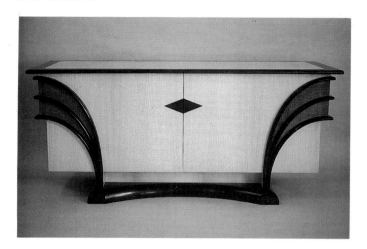

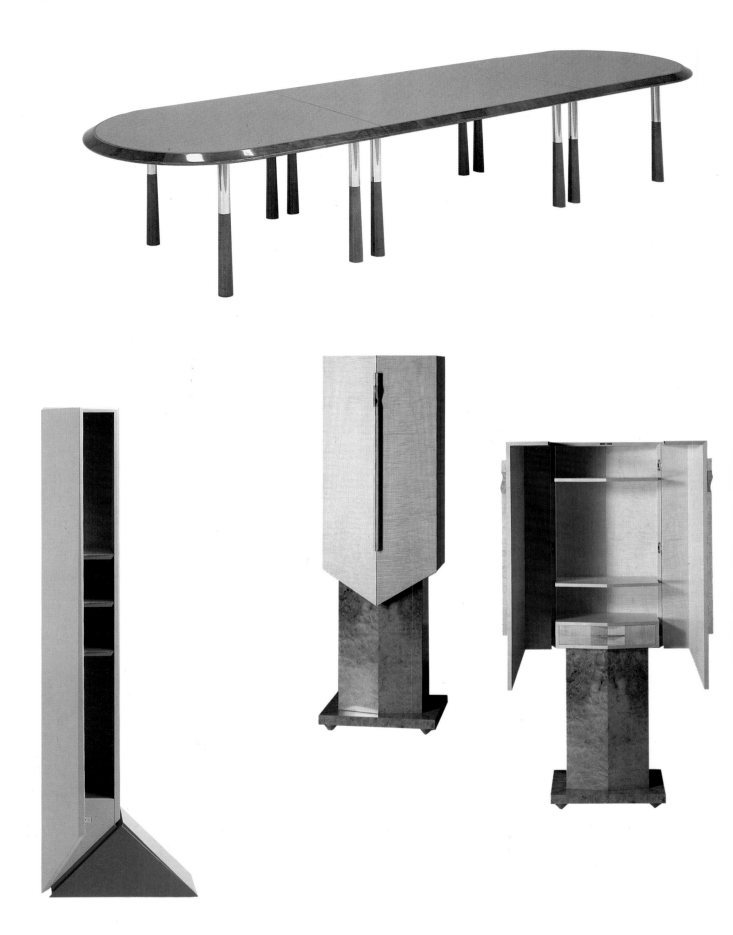

David Field

David Field served an apprenticeship as a mechanical engineer for Marconi Ltd., entering the Royal College of Art in 1969 to study industrial design. He quickly changed to furniture studies, not only because he decided he was more interested in furniture than kettles and fridges, but also because David Pye was one of the tutors. Ron Carter was another that he grew to respect, and he left the R.C.A. with a design philosophy greatly influenced by them both. For him an important part of that philosophy is that "Craftsmanship is an attitude of mind, a response to all materials. It means that you make well because the idea demands it — the idea simply won't come off if the object isn't well made — not just because you have a preoccupation with perfection." He believes that to achieve success one must keep the original philosophy firmly in mind, constantly seeking to fulfil and maintain it.

David has lectured at the Royal College of Art since 1979 and for many years has run his own workshop in London, producing individual furniture which has been exhibited all over Europe. He has served on both the Design Council and the Crafts Council, and acted as a consultant to the furniture industry in Great Britain and Hong Kong.

Corporate commissions are an important part of the work, alongside domestic furniture and speculative exhibition pieces. There is now a small team of craftsmen who work with him, and he would like to see the company become ". . . more efficient, more selective and more profitable so that everybody in the team has the opportunity to earn a good living from the activity without a reduction of standards or integrity."

Below: Dining table in pearwood — extends to seat from 6 to 14, leaves stored in support cabinet.

Top left: Boardroom table in silver grey maple and chromium with a grey leather top.
Drinks cabinet in sycamore and burr myrtle.
Drinks cabinet, open.
Bottom left: Lacquered pyramid cabinet.

Stephen Field

Cabinetmaker, Stephen Field spent two years studying fine craftsmanship and design at Rycotewood College, leaving seven years ago to work for himself making boxes and other smaller containers. Most of his work is based on the Sheraton period, a style he admires and follows closely in his own designs. The very high level of skill expected of a cabinetmaker is seen by Stephen as an important challenge to be met with every new project both as a craftsman and as a designer. The rewards he seeks are not in monetary terms, but in the ability of the craftsman to use rich, beautiful and exotic timbers, along with the satisfaction gained from the completion of a piece that fulfils his expectations.

Photograph frame in mahogany, veneered in amboyna, boxwood stringing with inlaid motif.

Champagne coolers in mahogany, veneered in amboyna, tulip wood crossbanding and ebony and boxwood stringing, with rosewood top and bottom. Lined with cork.

54

Malcolm Fielding

''Since being asked to make my first bobbins seven years ago, working on a small scale has been very attractive to me. My current designs are a mix of traditional and modern styles, using a wide variety of highly decorative and coloured woods.''
Malcolm J. Fielding

Collection of lace bobbins, including inlaid, spliced and slotted designs. Materials include ebony, boxwood, kingwood, laminated dyed veneers, gold beads. Size:3½'' (89mm) long x ¼'' (6mm) diameter.

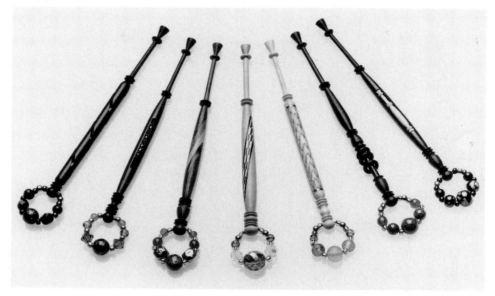

F.B. Design

Furniture maker and designer David Forrest runs his workshop from Alton in Hampshire and teaches design at the local sixth form college. His hall stand in ash and shot silk is a simple collaboration of materials and is formed to produce a functional yet striking piece of furniture.

Hall stand in ash and shot silk.

Photograph courtesy of
Frank Watson Photography.

Paul Fischer

This modern concert 8 string guitar, is one example of the work of luthier Paul Fischer. He makes copies of master instruments, such as this Baroque guitar by Antonio Stradivari, showing the elaborately carved soundhole. Also shown is the back view of another guitar of the Baroque period, made of ebony with boxwood inlaid lines and decoration on the neck. Apart from making guitars and lutes, Paul served a five year apprenticeship as a harpsichord, clavichord and spinet maker. He enjoys the craft and artistry of past masters and believes that instrument making has a tremendous advantage over other art forms — its ability to make music.

Modern concert 8 string guitar, the body of which is Brazilian rosewood, the soundboard of alpine spruce, the fingerboard of ebony and the rosette of Tunbridgeware.

Copy of a Baroque guitar by Antonio Stradivari. The body is made of sycamore, the soundboard of alpine spruce, the fingerboard, head and tuning pegs are of ebony.

Back view of a copy of a guitar of the Baroque period.

*Occasional table, pink and plain
sycamore veneers.*

Martin Fraser

In 1979 Martin Fraser attended a vocational course in fine craft and design at Rycotewood College in Thame, after which, in 1981, he started making furniture professionally from his workshop in Clwyd. At the moment most of his commissions are for public and private clients, but Martin sees a growing demand for prototype work and consultancy services to industry.

Adam Gallimore

Adam Gallimore studied advanced furniture design and construction at the London College of Furniture. He feels that wood still has many unexplored possibilities for innovative design due to its extraordinary texture and unique qualities. His work reflects his attempt to move away from the more recent trend of producing angular furniture.

Writing desk with four opening drawers, constructed in solid ash and veneered in burr oak. Solid ebony legs, feet, handles and mouldings.

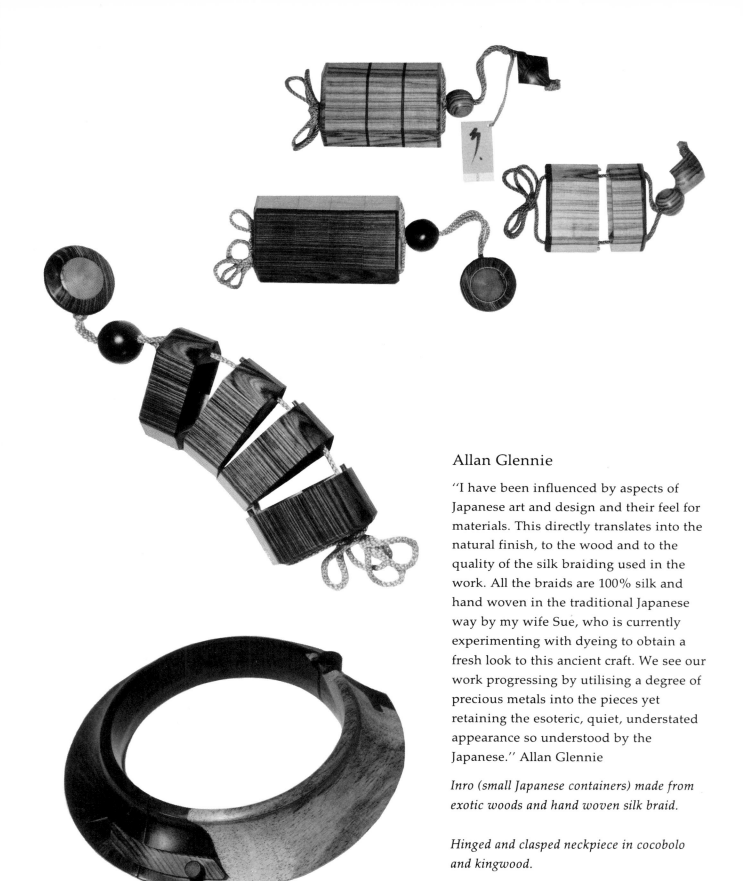

Allan Glennie

''I have been influenced by aspects of Japanese art and design and their feel for materials. This directly translates into the natural finish, to the wood and to the quality of the silk braiding used in the work. All the braids are 100% silk and hand woven in the traditional Japanese way by my wife Sue, who is currently experimenting with dyeing to obtain a fresh look to this ancient craft. We see our work progressing by utilising a degree of precious metals into the pieces yet retaining the esoteric, quiet, understated appearance so understood by the Japanese.'' Allan Glennie

Inro (small Japanese containers) made from exotic woods and hand woven silk braid.

Hinged and clasped neckpiece in cocobolo and kingwood.

Charles Good

Charles Good has been practising the ancient craft of marquetry for thirty-five years, endeavouring to modernise the techniques whenever possible. He has won the Marquetry Society's Rosebowl four times and instructs the local Harrow group.

"Forget Me Not"
"Five Waits"

Dennis French

The major influence on Dennis French's work has been the hand-craftsmanship learnt in the furniture making workshops at Chalford, where attention to detail and careful finishing were always of prime importance. He later diversified to making quality domestic woodware at an affordable price using machinery combined with hand finishing.

A collection of turned bowls spanning three decades. Lower picture: fruit bowl in English walnut inlaid with holly and ebony (1960). Below, left and right: salad bowl in burr elm (1970); salad bowl in English ash (1980).

Photograph courtesy of Leslie Seulfor.

Raymond Gonzalez

Whittling with penknives, razor blades and a blunt joiner's chisel was the way Ray Gonzalez began carving while still at school. His early working life included helping as an assistant in a bric-a-brac shop and was an introduction into the world of antiques, and, more specifically, the world of antique restoration. At the age of 19 he embarked on a career which now encompasses frame making, gilding, woodcarving and clay modelling.

During his apprenticeship with a London trade woodcarver's workshop, Ray studied at the City and Guilds School of Art in Kensington, and at evening classes. After working for other firms in London, he joined the sculpture and modelling department of M.G.M. film studio at Boreham Wood. Two years later he left to set up a small restoration business in partnership with a gilder, later relinquishing his share in the business to spend seven years as a craft teacher with mentally and physically handicapped and "difficult" children. During this period he maintained contact with a few clients and did selected work in his spare time. In 1984 Ray moved to the west country and re-established himself as a full-time woodcarver and gilder, making new pieces to original designs and reproducing the work of past exponents of the art and restoring antiques. His clients are antique dealers, interior designers, architects and private individuals. Ray works in partnership with his brother-in-law, Ben; one assistant and one trainee make up the staff of the workshop, in a steadily growing business.

18th century design of mirror frame demonstrating many of the standard elements of Rococco taste, carved in Quebec pine, gilded and toned.

Photographs courtesy of David Schooling.

Adaptation of a design by Matthias Lock, circa 1750, carved in limewood, water gilt and distressed. This sconce or girandole depicts the Aesop fable of the fox and the goat in the well.

Above right and below, detail of girandole.

Graydon Design

". . . I am not conscious of being influenced by any artist in particular, but I do gain inspiration from line and form, not necessarily confined to furniture, which combines a sense of space and function. I aim to produce dynamic and elemental furniture . . . and to be recognised as one of the top designers and makers of contemporary furniture in Britain."
Following a nine year career in market research, Neville Graydon founded Graydon Designs, making and designing furniture for both home and garden.

The Monochrome chair in stained ash.

The Mezzo table made in American black walnut with glass top.

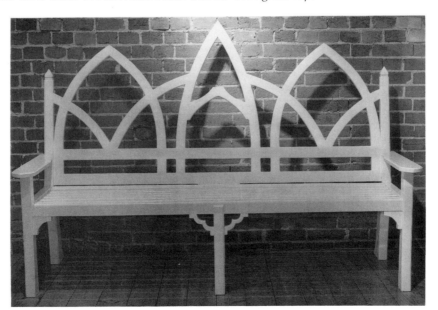

The Westminster Gothic garden seat made in chestnut, painted.

62

David Gregson

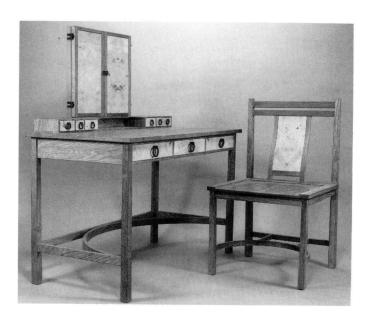

Dressing table and chair in brown oak and burr acacia with ebony details.

Sometimes one arrives at an occupation without really knowing how, and this is what has happened to David Gregson. With a degree in zoology behind him, he spent five years doing "nothing of any interest" except for the last two when he started, in his free time, to make or mend the odd piece of furniture and to do various other cabinet and carpentry work from an outhouse attached to his home. The process of making fascinated him. This spare time work developed and David has now been making furniture full time for the past ten years. Private commissions are his mainstay, encouraged by the local reputation he has gained by belonging to and exhibiting with the Norfolk Craft Society, Suffolk Craft Society and Norfolk Furniture Makers Association.

Director's desk in teak with ebony details.

63

Martin Grierson

In 1953 Martin Grierson graduated with distinction in furniture and interior design from the Central School of Art and Crafts in London and worked for a number of years with leading architects and interior design practices. In these early years he won several furniture design competitions including the Arflex/Domus European chair competition, the Timber Development Association Wooden Office Furniture prize and the Dunlopillo Design Award. Martin opened his own design studio in 1960 working on commissions for many large companies. In 1975, after many years of working within the limitations of mass manufacturing techniques he introduced the facility to make his own designs.

Martin, a Fellow of the Chartered Society of Designers, has served on Council and Professional Practice Boards. He has also been a member of the Design Council's Award Panel and Index Committee; the Craft Council's Index Selection Committee; and has served on the British Standards Committee for kitchen and office furniture. He is an external assessor to the furniture craft course at Buckinghamshire College and has, in the past, taught at Kingston, Birmingham and Leicester Polytechnics. He continues to work from his London based workshop for both private and corporate clients.

Library steps in mahogany.

Console table in natural oak with American black walnut features; top veneered with oak oysters.

Writing desk and chair in American black walnut and Maccasar ebony.

Chairman's dining suite table.

''Thai' cabinet veneered in Bombay rosewood with sycamore interior lining and ebony handles.

65

Martin Greshoff

Martin Greshoff has a diploma in design crafts
and no less than six City and Guilds
certificates in various wood related subjects.
Armed with all this knowledge Martin
recently started working for himself making
simple furniture with a geometrically based
influence. He intends to continue the
development of this style, making smaller and
more detailed items.

Chest of drawers in beech with ebony inlay.

Photograph courtesy of Robert Greshoff.

Ralph Hampton

"My long term goals are to get as close as
possible to the attitude that created Chinese
furniture, know it well, and then have fun
with it; to really know that what I do, I do
well, and is worthwhile; and to end my
economic oppression as a craftsperson who is
fully committed to quality, integrity and
making a statement in what I make." Ralph
Hampton

*Chair in oiled doussie. A close copy of a 17th
century Chinese original in the Victoria and
Albert Museum.*

Stephen Hallam

Stephen Hallam has recently completed his training. This consisted of three years at Rycotewood College, two brief spells working for established furniture makers and designers and a further three years working with David Field in London. Now specialising in private commissions, Stephen sees the future for his own small workshop being more involved in the contract furniture market, working in conjunction with architects and interior designers on special projects such as boardroom tables and reception desks. Although busy establishing his new business, Stephen finds time to return to Rycotewood, as a tutor this time, not a student.

Chair of stained birch plywood.

Lattice coffee table in ash with a glass top and magazine shelf.

Richard Foxcroft

Sixteen years ago when the great elm trees started dying of Dutch elm disease, fine artist Richard Foxcroft was in the process of buying his home, a run down timber framed house near Stevenage in Hertfordshire. With no knowledge at all he set about restoring the building, but very quickly realised that, although a crumbling wreck, it had been very well built and deserved to be put back together properly, even added to sympathetically. Cecil Hewitt's book *Development of Carpentry* was the main tutor, explaining the technicalities of timber frame construction. Armed with his newly acquired knowledge, and a passionate desire to keep the old elms as large as possible, they had been the biggest trees in Hertfordshire, Richard began again. Not only did he restore the house to its former glory, he added an extension and built a glass house in the garden. Commissions and enquiries followed, and he has been building and restoring timber framed houses ever since. In the course of one job large quantities of oak can be used, and to compensate for this the cost of replanting new oaks, which he does himself, is included in the price.

Richard has, up until now, worked only to commission, but he has just acquired a half acre site in Hertfordshire and is busy designing a new timber framed house. When all the houses in Hertfordshire are restored and there are no more sites for new buildings, Richard will have to move further afield, until then he enjoys his work although less labour and more design is his aim.

Unfinished extension to oak timber framed house.

Oak storey post with its wind bracing.

Glass house built of yew.

Ian Harris

"It is my belief that in many fields, from fashion to woodturning, the simplest, uncluttered designs are usually the best, with the simple classic lines making the highest impact." Ian Harris

"The Crucifixion" — bowl in burr elm, nails in yew with hawthorn crown stitched on with leather thong. Scorched rim. Courtesy of The United Reformed Church, West Kirby.

Photograph courtesy of Dave Flower.

Michael Henderson

Wood sculptor Michael Henderson has travelled extensively in Indonesia. Here, many local people believe that all nature is inhabited by spirits, and that forms made by man are able to represent these spirits and be powerful and useful. This particular aspect of Indonesian culture has been a close companion to Michael and he seeks to incorporate the spirit of the subject in his work and make the piece live. Initially trained as an architect, he has worked for fourteen years as a carver and sculptor, accepting commissions and selling his work direct to private clients and through galleries.

Hare in elm.
Toad in burr elm.

Nansi Hemming

Welsh lovespoon making is very much a traditional craft, and one which Nansi Hemming has learnt from her father. She now has a friend in her workshop learning in much the same way. She enjoys teaching when time and space permit, demonstrating and exhibiting as often as she can, sharing her knowledge with anyone who cares to ask. She feels that lovespoons have a very narrow traditional base and tries to add a little individuality, grace and beauty within the accepted scope of their design.

The dragon in pink ivorywood.
The ball and spiral in kingwood.
The Celtic loose links in zircote.   Photographs courtesy of Devon Commercial Photos.

Rocking chair – traditional style.
Photograph courtesy of D. Yaffe & Sons.

Smoker's bow chair in waxed beech and elm.
Photograph courtesy of Tony Griffiths.

Jack Hill

''I endeavour, unashamedly, to emulate the work of those unknown, unsung craftsmen from centuries past who, with simple tools and local materials met the needs of a large rural population. Like them, I begin out in the woods where I fell and cleeve ash coppice and beech, rough shaping with the draw knife and turning whilst still green before seasoning. By this means the natural resilience and strength of the living tree's fibres are preserved, even in slender components. Curved parts are steam bent and not laminated. Solid elm seats are hollowed by hand. Woven seats worked with rush or cord. It's slow, but it's very satisfying. And it's right.'' Jack Hill

Double bow Windsor chair in stained ash and elm. The three bead bulbous legs show a distinct north of England influence.

Photograph courtesy of Michael Chevis.

Suzanne Hodgson

Two years ago Suzanne Hodgson completed a two year course at the John Makepeace School for Craftsmen in Wood, and although she continues to study all elements of design, Suzanne is particularly interested in the Art Deco period, and feels that this may influence her work in the future.

Bowed shelving unit made with sycamore veneer and green-stained edging strip.

Jeremy Higson

Jeremy Higson began working for himself in 1983 after three years at Rycotewood College. This was the final stage in his formal education of working in wood which had been on-going since he was a small boy. He now works only to commission from his workshop in Evesham.

Family dining table, 3.8 metres extending to 5 metres. Quilted maple, sycamore and mahogany. The top is stained satinwood with a Greek key freize; the base is carved mahogany base on solid cast brass lion claw feet.

Luke Hughes

Luke Hughes is motivated by a passionate love of English furniture, particularly the pre-1750 period when academic theories began to dominate. The freshness and wit of early English furniture, he feels, was based on the direct involvement of the craftsmen with the design, long before the ravages of the Industrial Revolution prompted the emergence of the Arts and Crafts Movement.

The "Notery". A stand up writing desk in oak.

Office cabinet for box files made in English oak, with burr elm panels and rosewood details.

Mark Hutchins

Furniture maker and designer Mark Hutchins left the London College of Furniture in 1981, but it was not until 1984 that he began his own workshop in Havant, Hampshire. The work varies between commissions for private clients and sub-contracted work for large commercial concerns, a happy mix which Mark will continue to encourage. This dining-room suite underlines the philosophy of the workshop ''. All my designs are intended to be visually uncluttered, though they may be structurally complex and interesting. I like to use decoration, such as inlays, joint details, etc., where this enhances and emphasises the structure. I prefer to use solid hardwoods, mainly English, occasionally foreign, and sometimes rare or exotic veneers.''

Dining room suite in sycamore inlaid with rosewood, upholstered in leather.

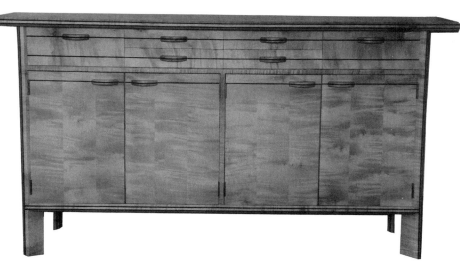

Robert Ingham

Robert Ingham has been the principal lecturer at the John
Makepeace School for Craftsmen in Wood, at Parnham since
1976. His personal aims are to blend fine craftsmanship with
design and to be recognised for his contribution to the
current movement fostering these aims. He believes that
success is the attainment of these personal objectives and lies
in the combination of personal standards of craftsmanship
and design that he is able to share with his students.

He was born in India, and moved to the U.K. at eleven years
of age. He was trained in craftsmanship at Loughborough
College, where very high standards were set by his two
mentors Reginald Henstock, lecturer in woodwork and Geoff
Hines, lecturer in metalwork. He later attended Leeds College
of Art to study design.

Robert's strong commitment to his students will ensure that
he stays teaching for some time to come, but he does cherish
a desire to set up his own workshop. In the meanwhile, in the
limited time available, he makes pieces for a small number of
exhibitions throughout the year, and for a few private clients.

*"Tower of Drawers" in yew and
burr madrone with burr elm feet.
Handles of rose quartz and gold
pins.*

*Jewellery chest. Bog oak frame
with burr elm panels. Trays of
ripple sycamore.*

"Wall of Drawers" ripple sycamore with titanium handles and detail.

Rachel Hutchinson

Rachel Hutchinson is an honours graduate in furniture design, and this dresser, designed in 1986, is her "Homage to William Burgess".

". . . I decided to retain the richness and geometry of his designs, but replaced the heavy, sometimes cumbersome weight of his work with a lighter, crisper, more refined imagery. This was executed in sycamore using combination of traditional hand crafted methods and the latest technology in C.N.C. computerised routing. Red and blue Boliva veneers are laminated below the surface of the board, the pattern being routed to different depths to expose each colour. The work surface is "Corian", a modern, durable material." Rachel Hutchinson

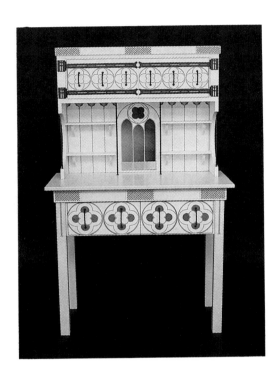

Neil Wyn Jones

Neil Wyn Jones used a grant from the Prince's Trust to good effect in 1982 when he set up his own workshop on completion of a furniture design and craftsmanship course at Liverpool Central College. One of Neil's long term goals is to furnish a whole room, but until and perhaps even after this commission has been achieved he is happy to continue designing and making individual pieces of furniture for his clients.

Music stand in rosewood.

"Happiness in Ebony."

Ernie Ives

Ernie Ives has worked with wood for over forty years, first as a boat builder, then as a craft teacher and now as a marquetarian. Ten years ago he became the editor of *The Marquetarian* bringing him into contact with other exponents of the art throughout the world. He enjoys trying new techniques, adapting old ones and constantly learning by experimentation, or from another craftsman, and the students he teaches in and around Ipswich and at summer school.

Five Degree Triangle
Sycamore and mahogany veneer.

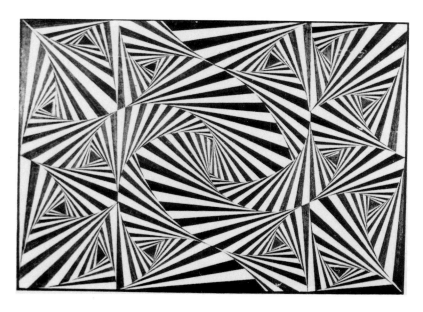

"Lazy Moments" (after Cooke), based on a Victorian painting. Considerable use has been made of unusual pieces of veneer to give texture and roundness to the dogs.

Les Jewell

Most of Les Jewell's work has been for the church. He has helped to furnish many cathedrals in England and America, in particular Washington Cathedral. Les loves his work, he is concerned only with the project in hand and finishing it to his own satisfaction, and he readily acknowledges that this makes him a very bad business man. A seven year apprenticeship has been followed by a lifetime of carving and at least thirty-four apprentices have been trained by Les in the thirty years he has been a woodcarver. When he is not decorating churches in the naturalistic way of his Gothic predecessors whom he so admires, Les sculpts in wood, teaches and lectures. He looks no further ahead than this and is "... quite content."

A section of a typical carving "Birds and grapes" English oak.

"The Thrush's Anvill" English oak.

"The Biter Bit". Buzzard, weasels and mice in oak.

Photograph courtesy of Freddie Collins.

Tom Kealy

The Somerset chair has become Tom Kealy's trademark. Even though he makes other furniture both singly and in small batch runs, it is the chair that he is remembered by. It started out as a desire to make a contemporary chair that he, being tall, would find more comfortable for long periods than the upright chairs of the Gimson era (which are a favourite of his) and yet still have a character of its own. Another quality it had to have was to employ simple, traditional methods using materials that were available locally and renewable in short periods of time. Thus it was that the Somerset Chair evolved after much sketching and many prototypes. Tom now makes them of local ash and willow in batches of twenty or thirty at a time and enjoys their simple appearance and the direct process involved in making them.

"Somerset" carver — ash and willow.
"Somerset" side chair — ash and willow.

Cecil Jordan

Cecil Jordan has been a professional turner and woodworker for over sixteen years. Before that he was a biological chemist and taught natural science and mathematics, working with wood during his free time. His only formal training was to spend a few weeks as a pupil of Douglas Hart, a well respected woodturner. The expertise has been gained through trial and error.

Over the years Cecil has acted as an assessor to the Worshipful Company of Turners, an advisor to museum purchasing panels and a national judge of woodturning. He is a member of the Gloucestershire Guild of Craftsmen, represented on the selected index held by the Crafts Council and has approximately twenty original designs selected by the Design Centre. He is a visiting tutor at West Dean College and Parnham House.

Of late, Cecil has been working in gold and antique ivory as well as wood, using an ornamental lathe for the fine and more complex detail. The gold is worked and hallmarked with his own goldsmith mark, replacing the small ''J'' or ''HCJ'' that is found on his wooden pieces.

Cecil's modest goals are for his work to continue to improve and to stand the test of time. Success, he feels, can be measured in two ways: if the work is commercial, then money must be the yardstick, but if it is artistic then it must have uncompromising quality.

Globe dressing table mirror set in burr wych elm.

82

Pieces for a dressing table — bog oak inlaid with burr oak.

Christening rattle in holly.

Covered box in Bombay rosewood with antique ivory inlaid in the form of a circular cribbage board.

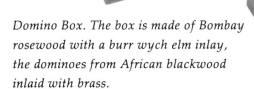

Domino Box. The box is made of Bombay rosewood with a burr wych elm inlay, the dominoes from African blackwood inlaid with brass.

83

Tobias Kaye

Tobias Kaye studied anthropology at Emerson College in Sussex before he started turning in 1979. He lives and works in Devon where his workload includes the making of architectural components, such as banisters and newel posts, bowl turning from homegrown hardwoods, as well as his more individual pieces for galleries and exhibitions. Cecil Jordan was a near neighbour when Tobias first became interested in woodturning, and was able to seek advice both technically and aesthetically. He acknowledges that this was very helpful.

The sounding bowls first appeared in 1987, along with a tape recording of the sonorous and meditative music made by the bowls. "My pieces are a developing search for harmony of form, seeking the right relationship of form to available material; to strive towards forms that speak or sound in their own right. This has led to the gut or wire strung sounding bowls where the inherent acoustic form is shown off by the notes struck or plucked from the strings." In his work, Tobias Kaye strives to make ". . . forms that touch people inwardly, remain beautiful with time and give joy."

Aeolian bowl No. 1 in olive ash, South American rosewood pegs, bronze wound string, brass bearings and enamelled copper wind hammers.

Sounding bowl No. 16 in holly, African blackwood pegs, bronze wound strings and copper/brass nuts.

Sounding bowl No. 22 in sycamore, bronze wound strings, brass bearings, African blackwood pegs and string hammers.

Burr oak pot.

Holly rollrim bowl.

Photographs courtesy of David Spires.

Roger Jeeves

Three years ago, Roger Jeeves, turned a lifetime's hobby into a full time occupation. As a keen Fenland wildfowler, Roger began to carve decoys for practical use, preferring them to the standard plastic ducks. As his interest developed he set about teaching himself to make the birds more realistic. He used books and illustrations by bird artists such as Tunnicliffe and began a collection of preserved birds, and parts of their anatomy, including bills and feathers. Local people, familiar with Roger's work, have been known to bring him traffic casualties for study. He has watched the way they fly, perch, land and feed trying to catch the essence of the bird in his work. As his skill has grown so have the commissions, coming from as far afield as America. Roger freely acknowledges that without his wife's patient help and support, her tireless dusting of his specimens, and perceptive critical eye ''. . . none of this would have been possible.''

Merlin.

86

Ring plover.　　*Roseat tern.*

Hen pintail.　　*Female kestrel.*

Photographs courtesy of Dave Parfitt.

David Linley Furniture

David Linley trained as a furniture designer and cabinet maker at the John Makepeace School for Craftsmen in Wood at Parnham House. He learnt the details of practical engineering and traditional methods for furniture and experimented with new ideas and materials. The increased demand for his work from customers in Great Britain, America, China, Japan and Canada led to the formation of David Linley Furniture Ltd. in 1985.

Matthew Rice, a co-founder of the company, has worked with David on many of the designs in the range they produce. Trained as a painter at Chelsea Art School, his watercolours are often a starting point for designing decorative finishes for the furniture.

They prefer to work with individuals and small workshops, rather than a factory based team, with the work being undertaken by selected craftsmen and specialists called in whenever necessary. Limited editions are signed and numbered and a few pieces are made for stock, but the majority of the work is for specific commissions, and include a 50 foot table for the Metropolitan Museum of Art in New York, decorative doors for the Berkeley Hotel, London, a suite of furniture for the St James' Court Hotel, London, and the design for the Linley piano for John Broadwood and Son, piano makers.

Venetian spiral staircase in oak, with marquetry and parquetry detail.

Console table in sycamore, pear and harewood.

Occasional table in pear and sycamore.

Occasional table in sycamore.

Desk in sycamore with ebony inlay.

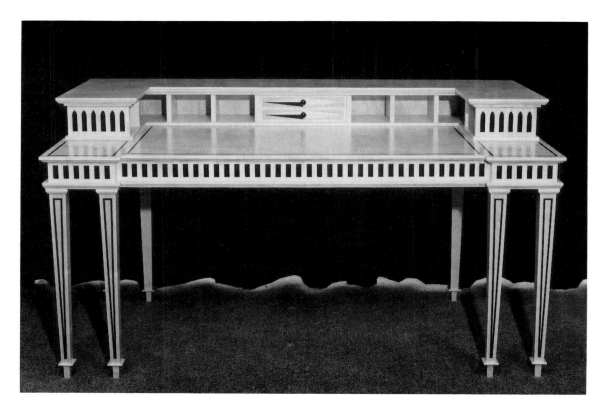

89

Kingswood & Burman Furniture Partnership

Following his four year career as a surveyor Mike Kingswood went to work for a cabinetmaker. He spent three years learning the trade and a further two running the workshop. In 1981 he began working for himself making furniture and fittings to commission. Lee Burman came to work for him in 1986, and it soon became apparent that Lee's design skills would add a new dimension to the business. The Kingswood and Burman Furniture Partnership is the new name for this team and they are currently working on many new ideas to compliment their existing range which includes the pieces shown here.

Occasional table in ebonised oak. (The side leaves and bottom drawer fold down to create the table top.)
Bureau in sycamore and lacewood with curved, drop front door.
Screen in English oak and stained glass.

Photographs courtesy of Dave Lewis.

Kodama

Born in the U.K. of Polish parents, Zyg Staniaszek took a degree in computer science, before working as a furniture maker at Kodoma Woodwork, eventually becoming the proprietor. Three years ago Huw Davies joined him as a designer and partner, Huw's degree was in three dimensional design. For logistical reasons, they originated a second company called D for design, run by Huw. Now it is possible to ask Huw for a design, and either commission the work from the sister company Kodoma, or take the design to another workshop. The partners have found that this eliminates the problem experienced by many smaller workshops of unpaid design work.

Table in sycamore and ebony.

Sideboard in natural and stained sycamore.

Ray Key

Ray Key became a full time woodturner in 1973. Although he had no formal training, he spent five years as a pattern maker's apprentice and turning was part of that discipline. From the age of seven the interest had been growing. He read every publication about turning that he could get his hands on and it became an all absorbing hobby in 1965 when he obtained his first lathe. His present output can be divided in two: half is table ware and the other half individual pieces of simple design and tactile quality that accentuate the beauty of the wood.

Ray's goal is to see woodturning given a much greater credence and acclaim in the same way that ceramics and glass are. The only way he sees this happening is for more turners to produce work of excellence, and to this end he will continue through seminars, workshops and writing to impart the information that he feels will help. He is a founder member of the Woodturners Association of Great Britain.

Enclosed rippled ash vessel.

Natural topped African blackwood bowl.

Natural edge burr oak dish.

92

Patrick Levins

Patrick Levins delights in the complicated detail arising from representing an 18th century scene in wood veneers. His work as a marquetarian is in complete contrast with his daily occupation as a joiner. After thirty years of less delicate woodwork he decided to fill his spare time in a way which would reveal the beauty of wood.

"Good companions."

"The craftsmen."

Philip Koomen

Philip Koomen trained at High Wycombe
College after studying applied social
science. He qualified as an Associate of the
Institute of Wood Science and was
awarded a scholarship from the Worshipful
Company of Furniture Makers. Philip
started working for himself in 1975 and
now runs a large workshop at Wheeler's
Barn, near Reading, employing three
craftsmen. He is sure that having people of
different talents working together produces
a dynamic and stimulating environment
that enables a wide range of work to be
undertaken, from single pieces to entire
rooms.

This television and video cabinet illustrates
Philip's aim to create furniture of
simplicity in line and form, using carefully
selected hardwoods to produce surface
decoration and pattern.

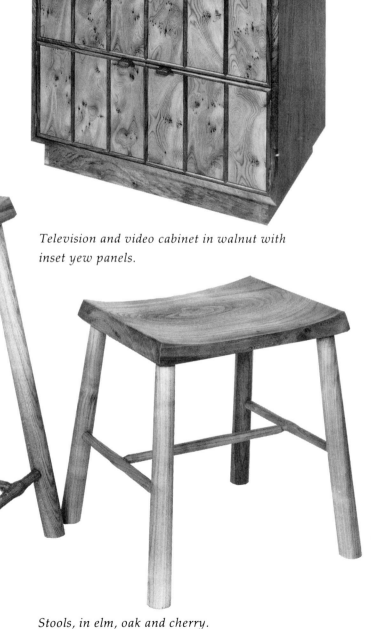

*Television and video cabinet in walnut with
inset yew panels.*

94

Stools, in elm, oak and cherry.

Laminated desk and chair in yew.

Laminated bathroom chair in ash.

Peter Kuh

Peter Kuh has had four years of practical training in workshops of various craftsmen, two years in America, followed by two with Alan Peters in Devon. For the next ten years he worked for himself, designing and making furniture. The origins of his style emanate from some of the more experimental, sculptural furniture being made in modern American workshops. He is a full-time lecturer at Rycotewood College, and continues to accept new, experimental commissions as time allows.

95

Richard La Trobe-Bateman

For the last twenty years Richard La Trobe-Bateman has been a furniture maker more concerned with structure than style. Now he is making bridges as well.
"A bridge offers an even clearer opportunity for exploring and demonstrating structure than furniture usually does. I use the triangle because it is the simplest inherently rigid shape."
Richard La Trobe-Bateman, *Contemporary Applied Arts exhibition leaflet, 1987.*

Sideboard. English oak, sawn, stained and lacquered.

Lasham Furniture Workshops

Three years at the London College of Furniture, followed by a further three working with a fellow craftsman is the way Hugo Egleston began what has now become fifteen years of furniture making. Commissions are his main source of work. He sees the future as an expansion of his present activities, developing his workshops and passing on his skills to a new generation.

Display cabinet on stand in cherry with black inlay.

96

Lucinda Leech

Lucinda Leech has run her own workshop in Oxford since 1977, designing and producing custom-made furniture in both British and exotic hardwoods. She regularly takes part in exhibitions and her clients vary from private customers to colleges, churches, businesses and galleries. As well as designing and making furniture Lucinda teaches, lectures and writes for the trade press. She spends a small part of each year travelling to research the forestry and timber trade, especially the rainforest areas. An award from the Worshipful Company of Furniture Makers enabled her to go to America and the Amazon; other destinations have included Malaya, Papua New Guinea and Australia. Lucinda finds that these expeditions have a stimulating effect on her work.

Dressing table in maple and ebony.

Drop leaf dining table in elm and sycamore.

Coffee table in American oak. End cone textured and stained black.

97

Ian Laval

Ian Laval's work is made entirely of locally grown, native timber which he processes himself. He is excited by the wealth of material obtainable from the whole tree when it is sawn traditionally for strong performance and appearance, including the book-matched veneers sawn from burrs, crotches and other features. He would like to see a much greater understanding of our native timber resources, believing that wood harvested and sawn in this way has so much more to offer.

The designs of the early 18th century and before are old favourites of Ian's and can be seen at his showroom.

Bureau in walnut, inlaid with holly, fall and drawers of sawn crotch veneers inlaid with holly. Handles, knobs and escutcheons cast in silver. (Two bureaux were made from the one walnut tree.)

Hall table in fumed oak, drawer of sawn crotch veneer, sycamore stringing.

Writing table in curly ash, walnut cockbeading and stringing.

98

Peter Lister

Peter Lister carves spoons for his clients to commemorate happy events in their lives: for love, weddings, christenings, or just to celebrate being a family. Some are carved with names and dates, others are self-explanatory as are the two shown here.

Entwined hearts in sycamore.

Two joined bowls with a pierced heart in cherry.

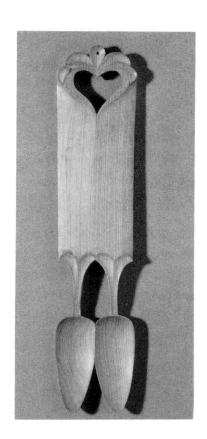

Nigel Lofthouse

Nigel Lofthouse's use of leather and painting began with nine years' designing fashion goods and fabric. His training in printing has given him a great interest in surface decoration, hand painting and engraving. He now sees his future work becoming more complex, combining many less common materials.

Tuareg throne chair. Made from turned oak and mahogany with hand painted natural cow hide, embellished copper and pewter panels, pure wool tassels with horn slides.

Trevor Lockie

"I have great admiration for carvings produced by the so-called 'primitive cultures' of the Northern Hemisphere, in particular the Palaeolithic hunter of Europe, and the Bering Sea Inuit. The early Japanese carvers who by their art encouraged the mind to focus on mere undynamic subjects of wildlife while retaining the highest degree of realism, are also important to me.

To be able to support my family in modest standards in one of the remotest and most beautiful areas in U.K., the north west coast of Scotland, and still find some unmeasured time to be able to observe and wonder in that place is my yardstick of success. But to achieve such an elevated position as that achieved by my Stone Age forebears, is, I feel, now impossible. We live under different constraints and the terms have changed so much they are hardly recognisable to the 20th century eye. Though I will still aim for a similar resolution of faithful image and praise drawn from my wild and immediate environment, I would like to add here and stress my lament at the almost total loss of respect for our partnership in the environment." Trevor Lockie

Human skull in Ceylon ebony, 5cm.

Slug and apple in ebony, pequia, briar and laburnam, 4.5cm.

100

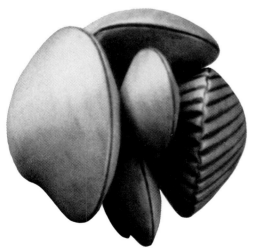

Snake and apple in rapala, 35cm.

Crab in shell in lignum vitae, pequia and stag's horn, 18cm.

Cluster of shellfish in boxwood, 4.5cm.

101

Michael Lowe

"In common with any musical instrument maker my main concern is with the sound of my finished instruments. I see my job primarily as making a tool with which the musician may create his art, and to that end I must try to ensure that my lutes possess a wide expressive capability comprising such things as a good range of volume and tone colour, and evenness of response throughout the instrument's range. The musician must feel that the instrument helps rather than hinders his intentions in performance. As a maker of historical instruments, however, all my efforts to achieve these ends must be within the conventions established by the makers of the past. Since the music which is to be played on my instruments is music of previous ages, my aim is to come as close to the historical models as my researches and understanding will allow — no easy thing, given the very complicated history of the lute." Michael Lowe

A rose from a Renaissance lute.

11 course French lute, back of figured sycamore and pear, neck and peg box in ivory and ebony.

Peg box and bass rider of a 13 course German Baroque lute in pearwood, carved and stained.

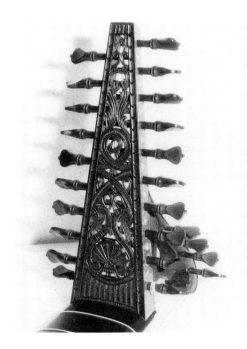

102

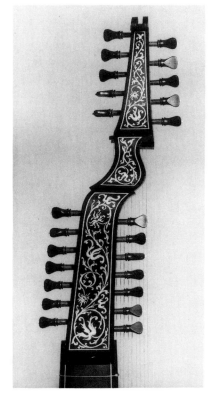

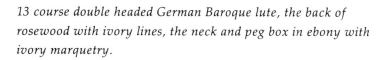

13 course double headed German Baroque lute, the back of rosewood with ivory lines, the neck and peg box in ebony with ivory marquetry.

John MacFarlan

John MacFarlan spent his leaves studying furniture making in a cabinet maker's workshop. When he left the navy 20 years ago, he worked for a year in forestry before starting his own business making furniture. He designed The Longwood Furniture Range especially for his clients, who are, in the main, local people, and at present is working on a new style of dining room furniture which will be promoted both locally and nationally. With the help of his wife, and stubborn persistence, he has managed to maintain financial stability although this is still a major concern. His future plans include experimenting in sculpture with a view to decorating his furniture.

Walnut chair and writing table, sycamore and lacewood inlay.

104

David Marshall

Living in the beautiful Welsh countryside at Betws-y-Coed, David Marshall,
although qualified as an art and craft teacher has been working in wood for the
past twenty years. Most of his work is commissioned because he does not find
rural Wales the best market for unusual speculative pieces of furniture, which he
admits he would like to do more of.

*Gazebo at Trecastell Hall, Anglesey. 12ft (3.65m) high, 10ft (3.05m) square. Oak frame, laminated roof
curves. Treated and painted softwood trellis.*

Chair in English holly.

John Makepeace

"It is of great value to look outside for inspiration, values and direction."

John Makepeace

To this end John Makepeace has studied and absorbed the teachings and influence of many specialists and practitioners including William Morris' thoughts on the quality of life and work, David Pye's teachings on design and philosophy, Norman Leyland's directions for management, economics and education along with the ideas of Norman Foster and Frei Otti on architecture and structures. His extensive travels to Scandinavia, Italy, Africa, U.S.A., India and Japan have also had a significant effect on his work.

Continued survival, development and growth are John's own measure of success. He attributes it to a gradual building of reputation, an outward looking attitude for inspiration and direction, and the implementation of change

106

through business and education. These factors are only made possible by collaboration with teams of specialists.

"The objectives are clear: increased appreciation of the potential qualities of individual furniture, so that both patrons and makers become more courageous; to produce work which is of its time, not so much stylistically as by a self-reliant and aesthetic expression of function, material and method; and to re-establish volume furniture making and building methods in harmony with the natural environment for the 21st century. Achieving some of them will take a life-time."

John Makepeace

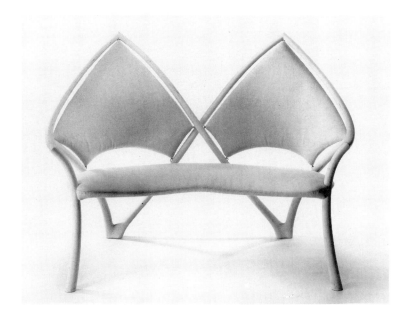

'For Eloquent Discussion' Laminated, carved and scrubbed English oak with canvas cover.

Dining table. Laminated, braced structure in cherry, spliced and carved. Matched wenge veneers for the table top.

John Makepeace
Continued from page 107

Side table in scrubbed burr oak and burr elm.

Chair in Indian rosewood and desk in thuya burr and cast bronze.

Writing table and chair. Ripple sycamore with fawn leather. The table top incorporates a pair of drawers.

Bert Marsh

"My principal objectives are the creation of stimulating art forms by wood turning, and revealing the hidden beauty of natural growth. I select my material from a wide variety of bland and exotic timbers, paying particular attention to natural defects, discolouration, and grain malformations. Sensitive turning exposes the textures, colours and patterns which are enhanced by meticulous finishing. Exciting geometric designs are achieved by the cutting, joining and carving of turned sections. Many of my vessels are functional, but I would prefer them to be judged for aesthetic elegance, craft and creativity and hope that in time they will become valued collectors' pieces."

Walnut bowl, made from six smaller bowls.

Three holm oak vases.

Spalted beech vase.

109

John Mackie

John Mackie was originally inspired by Art Deco objects and early American juke boxes, but has recently moved to making more classically derived pieces in mahogany and finely burred veneers. John was trained as an electronic technician as well as a commercial and industrial photographer, so perhaps it is not too surprising that he now makes these Art Deco style radios as part of his range of "room accessories".

Art Deco style radios in walnut.

Gordon Marsh

Successfully completing a diploma course in furniture production at Buckinghamshire College two years ago, Gordon Marsh began working for himself in Harrogate, North Yorkshire. Being fairly new to the life of a professional craftsman Gordon's initial ambition at the moment is to make a success of what he is doing, in building a clientele for whom he can design and make furniture.

Display case made from solid ripple sycamore. The right-hand door is hinged conventionally, the left two are hinged and sliding.

110

Pithill chair in ash, painted.

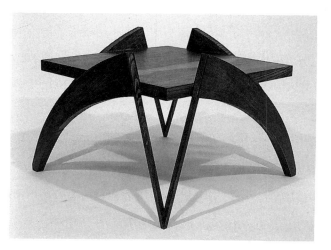

Low table in stained ash.

Folding chair in stained ash.

Guy Martin

Sculpture played an important part in the formative years of Guy Martin. Not only was his father a sculptor, but in 1969 Guy obtained an arts degree with honours, specialising in sculpture, at St Martins School of Art in London. He then became assistant to the sculptor Anthony Caro for two years. For the next ten years he followed many occupations, including diving, photography and fabric design, returning to work for Caro in 1981. This latter period with the sculptor was the catalyst, and in 1984 Guy began making furniture. He now works in Devon producing items made in small batch runs as well as accepting commissions. His distinctive furniture can be seen both at local and national exhibitions. Guy teaches design at Parnham House, and believes ''. . . that the future holds a richness yet undreamed of with the marrying of skills, aesthetics and cultures within a technological age.''

Trevor Mayhew

Trevor Mayhew is a graphic designer whose ambition is to move towards earning his living from carving full time. Trevor enjoys mixing timber species in one piece, sometimes adding metals, shell or minerals, hopefully conveying in the design a little of the sense of magic that he feels is contained within Nature's designs, whether attractive or unsettling. This method is well illustrated here in his *Jack in the Green* carved from willow burr with an inset glass eye. The ivy surround is of green stained lime, the hemispheres are lime and the framing split willow branches.

Alec McCurdy

''I have experienced the joy of working with wood and tools from an early age. While working with Stanley Davies in 1953 and Edward Barnsley in 1953 to 1954, I was inspired by the integrity of their workmanship and the joy in the making of traditional furniture to the best possible standards. Hence, I am now making individual pieces of furniture from solid English timbers. They incorporate where appropriate, the richly figured wood from the crown or crotch of cherry and walnut trees, in particular for the panels of my cabinets.
As to the future, should a dedicated craftsman ever wish to retire?, I don't, for sure.'' Alec McCurdy

Walnut music cabinet, with framed and panelled back. The top fall opens to reveal shelves for sheet music, the drawer houses cello bows or tapes, etc, and the bottom shelves for records and scores.

Henry Mein

Without formal training, Henry Mein has had a lifetime interest in three-dimensional sculpture. His earliest work dates from 1939, and he still has the piece that he carved in the occupational therapy unit of Horton Emergency Military Services Hospital whilst recovering from war wounds in 1944/5. After the war Henry qualified as an architect and has until recently been a senior partner of his firm, finding time for his carving whenever he could. Happily, he is now a consultant to the partnership and to all intents and purposes is a full-time sculptor.

"Magi", oak

Photograph courtesy of Middletons Photographers.

Martin Midwood

Martin Midwood, not surprisingly, draws his inspiration from monuments, castles, ruins, standing stones and rock formations. This high backed throne chair, has ceramic legs which are modelled in sections and hollowed and assembled after firing. An open-bodied clay is used with added grog to give a coarse texture and dry glazes give a range of matt colours which are designed to emphasise those found in the wood. A split oak roof beam makes up the back rest, while the seating sections are cut down from floor joists which are secured to cross spars by pegs with turned heads.

Neville Neal

"Ernest Gimson has been the major influence on my work. I was trained by one of his craftsmen and my whole working life has been spent in making chairs mainly to Gimson's fine designs. My aims have been to maintain the high standard of craftsmanship set by the Cotswold Group and to refine the chairs so that, to quote one commentator, 'They are as traditional as time, yet absolutely perfect in the most modern of homes.' Since 1966 I have been assisted by my son, Lawrence and, as demand continues, with the chairs as popular as ever, the future of the craft seems assured." Neville Neal

Spindle back rocking chair in oak.

Photograph courtesy of the Rural Development Council.

Ladderback rocking chair in ash.

Photograph courtesy of Mike Brown.

114

Dressing cabinet, made from pitch pine with a mirror-fronted cupboard and two drawers beneath.

Dresser, made from American cherry with Breche Nouvelle marble top.

Nielson and Nielson

"Our work is an investigation into the use of materials and structure to make furniture that has a decorative quality gained from the way it is constructed, rather than applied decoration, and a presence that is neither jarringly modern nor seemingly antique. Most furniture is made from a combination of materials, which contrast and compliment each other. These materials range from hardwood and marble to painted metal and concrete, but our work is predominantly in hardwoods. We have experimented successfully in the use of colour washes and painted finishes on small areas, to give emphasis to the structure."

　　　　Antonios and Ruth Nielson

"Melpo" settee, made from maple with painted details.

Hall table in English walnut with ebony detailing.

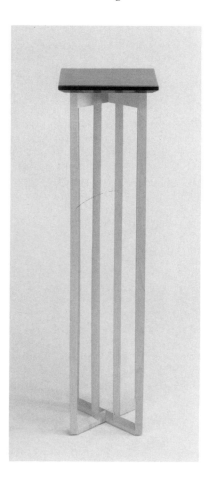

Plant stand in sycamore and ebony.

Writing desk in walnut.

Matthew Morris

Matthew Morris graduated from the furniture making and design course at Buckinghamshire College of Higher Education with distinction. Before finishing his course, he was commissioned to furnish a house in Cambridgeshire. "... I went for a clear design when at college which was criticised by some lecturers for being staid and traditional. However, then as now, I am trying to achieve classical furniture of timeless quality, that does not ignore the past. I want to produce furniture away from the obsession with trying to be absolutely different — today I carry on in the same vein.

"I do not believe in the country craftsman quietly working his wood and living, maybe a comfortable life, but not luxurious. The craftsman is far too content to declare his art as a labour of love and this is where I disagree.

"To me, furniture is my business and must be commercial. Therefore my furniture is realistic in design and cost which is why I want to see it in everyone's home, regardless of financial status. Perhaps I follow Terence Conran's directives, for I plan to open shops of my own, or at least see my work on show in the top retail outlets."

Dining chair in walnut.

Display cabinet in walnut.

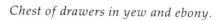

Chest of drawers in yew and ebony.

Lucie McCann

Four years ago Lucie McCann gained an honours degree in three dimensional design at Kingston Polytechnic. Since then she has been designing furniture at her studio in Guildford trying not necessarily to change the face of furniture design today, but to re-introduce an element of the decoration and beauty of the classical form into furniture which she would eventually like to see work its way into mass production.

A three seater bench in European walnut with a slatted seat and classical motifs in the back.

Liam O'Neill

Liam O'Neill could be called a career woodturner, at the age of 19 Liam served an apprenticeship for four years with John Shiel at Bagenalstown. It was during these years that he met Maria Van Kesteren, a Dutch woodturner whose work was to have a profound effect on Liam's work. In 1980, after seeing American woodturners at work at an International seminar, he decided to set up his own studio in Shannon. He later founded the Irish Woodturners' Guild and he teaches and exhibits a great deal in Britain adding to the British scene, as well as teaching abroad.

Natural edge bowl in yew burr.

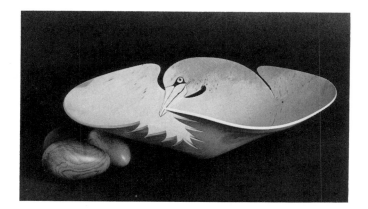

Nest series, sycamore with acrylic paint.

Liz and Michael O'Donnell

"Since 1981 Liz and I have collaborated in the making of our pieces, working only in fresh sawn, non-commercial timber from Caithness, i.e. trees which have been blown down in the wind or cut down to make way for houses. These are mainly sycamore and beech, which, being very plain timbers, have led us away from the natural edge bowl to decorating simple shaped bowls by carving and/or painting. The early ones were more geometric in design, but living in the country, on the north coast of Scotland, and being considerably influenced by our environment, these evolved into bird forms."   Michael O'Donnell

Bird series, ganet in beech with oil paint, ganet in sycamore.

Plank back chair, limed oak.
Designed by Robert Williams.

*This is one of Pearl Dot's best
known designs and considered to
have contributed much to their
success.*

Pearl Dot

Robert Williams, Stephen Hounslow
and Chris Rose work together with
six assistants designing and making
for architects, churches, and
corporate and private clients. All
furniture from the Pearl Dot
workshop is "signed" with a small
inlaid disc or "dot" of mother of
pearl.

The three partners provide an
insight to their design philosophy:
"The improvement of the quality of
people's environment in terms of
design, and quality of making and
materials is something I continually
aim for. I believe people's thinking
and behaviour are affected by their
surroundings and I want the widest
number of people to benefit from my
efforts in this direction. Hence, given
a design I think is good, I will try to
make it as accessible as possible. I
am 'anti-elitist' in craft matters."
Robert Williams.
"The challenge of widely different
types of private commissions over

Directional table in sycamore.
Designed by Chris Rose.

the years are all influencing my current approach to producing refreshing, contemporary designs that are well produced products for direct sale — and which are affordable. I have always been interested in natural and invented pattern and structure, and I am currently am developing drawings and finished designs on a computer system which allows my various approaches to design to be combined with working drawings and client presentations." Chris Rose

"Undoubtedly, one of the greatest influences on my life and work has been the Bible. From this stems a belief that the Creation is both divinely ordered and sustained. This belief does not imply that I am a better or more talented designer than any other, but does demand that I strive to reflect a divine order in all I do and make." Stephen Hounslow

Photographs courtesy of Jonathan Tickner.

Organ screen in English oak with stained and gilded detail. Designed by Stephen Hounslow from a concept by Richard Woods the organ builder.

Plan chest in grey "grain stained" ash. Designed by Pearl Dot.

121

Trevor Oliver

A member of the Society of Designer Craftsmen, Trevor Oliver has worked with wood for the last twenty years. He spends most of his time passing on his skills to the next generation as a craft, design and technology teacher at Looe School in Cornwall. When he is not teaching, Trevor is designing and making furniture that he feels is peaceful to live with. He works to commission and for exhibitions and one day hopes that this will become a full time occupation.

Chest in English sycamore.

Photograph courtesy of Clemens Photography.

Jim Partridge

Jim Partridge has moved outdoors. After eight years making his very own style of bowl he is now making furniture and bridges with a definite rustic quality in keeping with their surroundings. This foot bridge in oak was made for Northern Arts and the Forestry Commission and is situated in Grizedale Forest in the Lake District. Jim envisages that half his work will now be outdoors, working in partnership with Liz Walmsley, and the other half, making bowls.
He learnt his craft at the John Makepeace School for Craftsmen in Wood and continues to pass on his ideas, as a visiting lecturer, to students of three-dimensional design courses.

Gilded, bleached burr oak bowl.
Footbridge. Oak logs.

Tony McMullen

Tony McMullen served his apprenticeship in the furniture making industry in the late sixties. This continued for five or six years, after which he began to run two careers together. The first as a furniture designer and maker, the second as a tutor in these subjects at Birmingham Polytechnic where, among other students, he taught Freddie Baier. Tony has no intention of giving up his part time post to devote all his time to furniture making, as he feels that his contact with the young people at the college gives him the stimulating environment he needs for his work. Taking part in various exhibitions up and down the country provides him with much of his work which is domestic furniture for private use rather than the larger pieces for corporate clients. During the college holidays Tony employs one of the students, giving them an insight into the working life of a designer/maker.

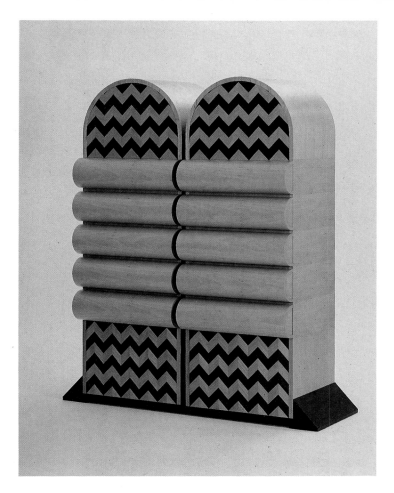

Twin chest of drawers made from plywood laminates and precoloured veneers.

Extending table made from sycamore and stained mahogany; seats 4 to 8 people.

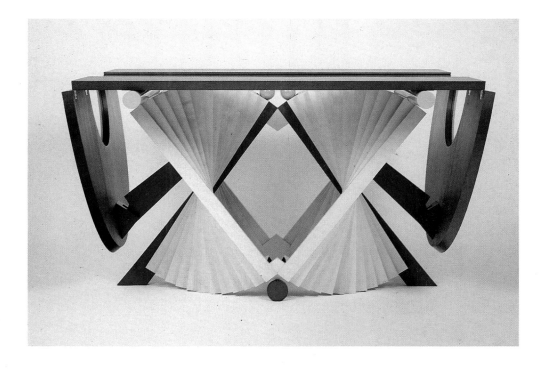

123

"Merlin" English walnut, limewood, elm, silver, gold, antique ivory, garnet, coral, pearls, quartz, amber and resin — In the Arthurian legends Merlin was teacher and magician to the king. He guided Arthur throughout his life trying to avert the inevitable end of the Round Table and Camelot.

"The Acrobat" English walnut and limewood.

Ian Norbury

"The richness of an artist's work reflects the richness of his mind, and consequently the selection of that work by a buyer reflects the richness of his taste. By constantly absorbing a wider variety of information and channelling it into my work I try to make every aspect of it richer, more stimulating and exciting, hopefully achieving the elevation of my work, both artistically and financially." Ian Norbury
"The richness of an artist's work reflects the richness of his mind, and consequently the selection of that work by a buyer reflects the richness of his taste. By constantly absorbing a wider variety of information and channelling it into my work I try to make every aspect of it richer, more stimulating and exciting, hopefully achieving the elevation of my work, both artistically and financially."

"The Magician" English walnut, boxwood and gold.

"Dominion", limewood — Dominion is the artist's interpretation of Man's dilemma in the ever increasing need to conserve our planet. It symbolises the delicate balance between Man and Nature with the life of the bird totally within Man's power, to crush and extinguish life or to liberate and protect. This is emphasised by the way that the fingers of the hand are threaded through the wing feathers of the dove, making the bird's life seem all the more delicate and precious. The title is taken from the bible text, Genesis Chapter 1, verse 26 — "And God said, Let us make man in our image, after our likeness: and let them have dominion over the fish of the sea, and over the fowl of the air, and over the cattle, and over all the earth, and over every creeping thing that creepeth upon the earth."

"The Lord of Misrule" English walnut and gold — The Lord of Misrule was the director of the festival of the twelve days of Christmas. This was called the Feast of Misrule and was derived from the Roman Saturnalia.

Ian Norbury

Woodsculptor Ian Norbury works from his studio and gallery in Cheltenham. He accepts no commissions, preferring instead to generate his own ideas. Every avenue and whim that he has relating to his work is fully exploited, including the use of a wide variety of materials as appropriate. Ian considers success in his work to be the attainment of the level of perfection to which he aspires, but feels that this will never happen. Nevertheless he willingly admits that what financial success he has achieved are attributed to the help of his wife and his bank manager, who have encouraged him and enabled him to spend his days striving for that perfection.
His work is sold through his gallery and his annual one-man exhibitions.

"Pan", burr elm and antique ivory — In early Greece Pan was depicted as a handsome youth, only later acquiring the attributes of a goat. He pursued the Arcadian nymph, Syrinx, who took refuge in the River Ladon where she was changed into a reed, from which Pan made his pipes.

Dining Table and Chairs. Sycamore with split cane chair seats. Designed by Garry Olson and made in partnership with David Bell.

Garry Olson

Garry Olson, an ex-patriot Australian, began his woodworking career making pine beds with a colleague in a cellar, and from this association the Sawyer Furniture Making Co-operative was formed in Didsbury, Manchester, working with other makers. 1986 saw the purchase and renovation of the Stoney Lane workshop and gallery where he was able to work either individually or with his partner David Bell on commissions and speculative pieces for display in the showroom. In 1989 Garry became the sole occupier of the premises and looks forward to continuing the development of both his own reputation as a maker, and that of his showroom and gallery where he envisages holding an annual exhibition.

Chest of drawers in English walnut with oak and cedar of Lebanon interior.

Photographs courtesy of Lighthouse Studio.

Alan Peters

"Success is achieving those goals, however modest, that you, and you alone, have set. My own goal back in 1962 was to attain a reasonable standard of living for myself and my family by working to my designs and my standards without either having recourse to other forms of income such as teaching, or turning my workshop into a production sweatshop. Coupled with this was a desire to make my work available to a wide cross-section of society and not principally to the wealthy. I also wanted to create workshop training opportunities in order to repay the debt for what I had personally received. Helped along largely by changes in social conditions, over which I had no control whatsoever, a patient, tolerant and thrifty wife and a certain dogged stubborness on my part, this is largely what I have done.

"I am still influenced by the Arts and Crafts pioneers of the last century and the early 20th century exponents of the modern movement, for I still believe passionately in honesty to materials and construction and, despite the many

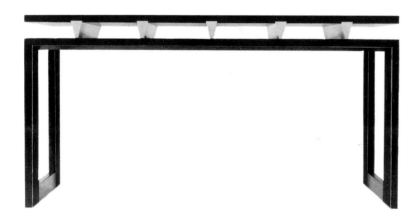

Serving table in Indian padauk with sycamore cross members.

Nest of five tables in Macassar ebony veneers on medium density fibreboard with edges of steam bent white rippled ash.

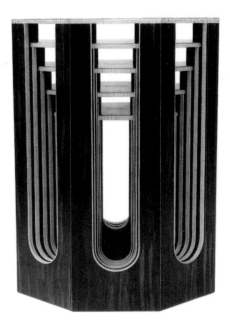

Dining table in white sycamore; centre panel of top and domed section of base in slate grey dyed veneers.

hours I might devote to a piece, I like to think it still represents a straightforward and logical use of materials and construction techniques, where economy of effort and time still has its place. I also believe strongly in the value of hand skills in my work, but hopefully doing so with a degree of restraint and repose, and always in the context of the logical construction of the piece. I draw much of my inspiration from my travels abroad, particularly from my visits to the Far East, but it is the simple vernacular architecture and folk crafts made by craftsmen over the centuries without any pretension that impress and stimulate me wherever they are found.

"Having achieved my initial ambitions, the future presents new challenges, for no creative person can stand still or retire, and I am no exception. Freer now of some of the financial and family commitments of earlier years, hopefully I can now reap the benefits of those years of experience and produce my best work yet." Alan Peters

Serving table in wenge with drawer fronts of yew.

Storage cabinet in wych elm with handles and base of wenge.

Dining table to seat ten. The top is made from one exceptional board of wych elm shaped to a concave curve in its length to echo the inner curves of the two sections.

129

Leslie Plail

Les Plail has been sharing a workshop in Bromley, Kent with John Wilsher since completing two years as a mature student at Rycotewood College in Thame, five years ago. Whilst most of his work is to commission, Les would like to continue to develop his own style which he feels is reminiscent of the simpler ideas of the 1930's, such as these low tables in ash solids and veneer. The design is part of a series based upon geometric shapes: circles, squares and triangles supporting the overhanging top. The table is in two halves that may be used separately, or together as one large table.

Seal table.

Low tables in ash.

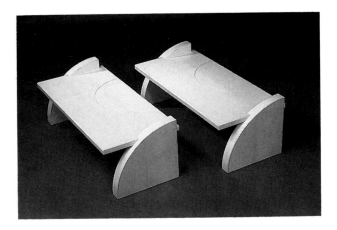

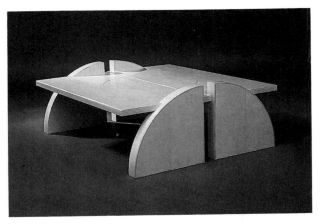

Derek Pearce

Derek Pearce's work displays an element of humour, and looking at the varied occupations that Derek was engaged in before furniture making it is perhaps not surprising. His background stems from a family of master builders. He went to art college in Stourbridge, after which he worked in an avant garde street theatre. This was followed by a period of further education at Nottingham University where Derek qualified as a teacher. He later began writing music for theatre, films and radio, and with all these interests he still returned to the woodworking tools that he was given at the age of 10. These have been supplemented over the years with chain saws and other tools as his awareness of other materials and new techniques has grown.

David Pye

"What I seek to achieve in my own work is to do a bit better. I set great store by the surface finish and the feel of the wood and also by the cleanness of the cutting: all the arrises should be clean and all the curves should be fair, and so on. If you take enough trouble, endless trouble, that part turns out reasonably well – not every time, admittedly, but fairly often. It is not the workmanship that is so difficult, but the design. That never gets easier. In design, very small differences make all the difference. The difference between the thing which sings and the thing which is forever silent is often very slight indeed. Why one should feel impelled to go on trying to make something which sings I really do not know, but that apparently is the fate of artists in however small a field. Perhaps in the end we do it in the hope that in time to come someone's eye will light when they see a thing we have made and they too will feel the same impulse. Perhaps all good art has been addressed to a generation still unborn." David Pye. (Extract from selector's essay, *The Makers Eye*, exhibition catalogue, Crafts Council, 1981.)

Kingwood needle case, Jamaica satinwood lid. Kingwood box, wild service tree lid.

Photo courtesy of Crafts Council

Professional Woodworkers

Jonathan Hawkes was first introduced to wood while still at
Eton, where he won the school's woodworking prize for an
oak guncase. His first commission was a pine table for a
friend's mother when he left school, followed by work from
other family friends. Here the career in woodwork becomes
varied: from 1972 to 1984 Jonathan did many things, he
washed plates in France, manufactured and developed
skateboards in London, toured America, and made furniture,
eventually settling down to form his own Wiltshire based
company, Professional Woodworkers. Jonathan enjoys what
he calls the phenomenal versatility of wood and the new and
different problems it constantly presents.

Chaise-longue made in tiger maple and gold silk taffeta, a pair of which now reside in a palace in Istanbul.

Spiral dining table made in solid mahogany cut from one piece of wood with ebony dot detail, topped with oval shaped bevel edged glass.

Photographs courtesy of Phil Bergan.

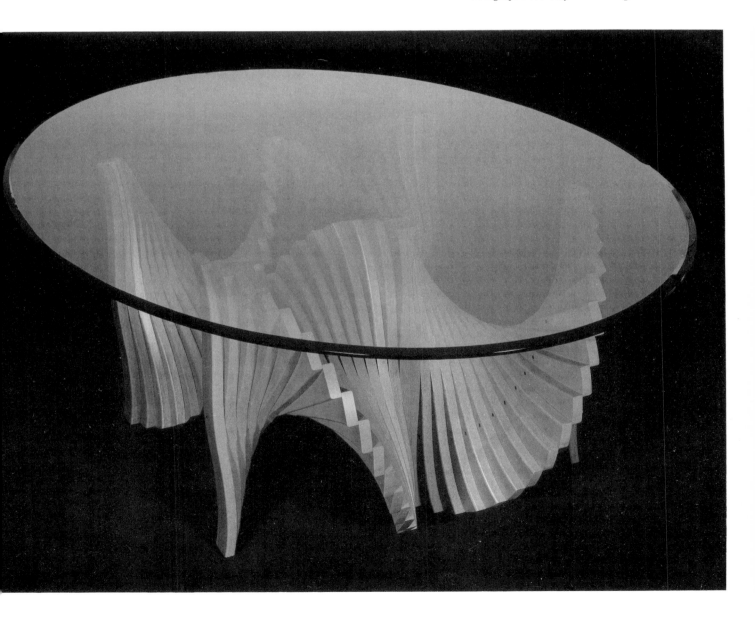

Brian Reeves

Brian Reeves has been working with wood over twenty years, but only began seriously to earn a living from this activity after completing a course at Rycotewood College three years ago. He makes reproduction furniture, favouring the Queen Anne period which enables him to use the wood he most likes, walnut. His workshop is based in Hampshire, where he enjoys working alone, "... deriving a great deal of satisfaction from producing a piece from start to finish."

Queen Anne style kneehole desk in walnut.

Queen Anne style bureau in walnut.

134

Trunnion boxes. 4" (100mm) high in laburnum, yew, hornbeam, walnut, box and fruit wood.

Dave Regester

Degrees in English and philosophy are not necessary qualifications for a woodturner, but Dave Regester has these as well as a family with a long history of woodworking, and this is where his interest in wood originates. It seemed to him to be the natural way of making a living.

Using only home grown timber, the majority of his work is utilitarian ware, but when he is not making salad bowls and other kitchen utensils he uses the same discipline to create his more decorative pieces including these flights of fancy which he calls his "Trunnion Boxes".

John Sagar

It wasn't until he was 29 that John Sagar discovered that furniture making was for him. He then studied as a mature student at Rycotewood College, and spent a further year learning the trade with a Nottinghamshire cabinetmaker. Books and exhibitions have allowed him to follow the work of contemporary furniture makers, including Alan Peters and Richard La Trobe Bateman. John has, for the past ten years, worked mainly to commission.

Dining table in English oak. The design was inspired by the work of Edward Barnsley. The wishbone stretcher was the answer to the customer's need for maximum leg-room.

Humpback pintail drake carved in the style of the Ward Brothers.

Mallard duck carved in jelutong, fully feather textured and painted in acrylics.

Robert Ridges

The sea had always been in the blood of Robert Ridges. At seventeen he went to sea, working his way through the ranks to become a Master Mariner, meaning that he was qualified to take any vessel anywhere in the world. His spare time on board was occupied with making model ships and painting watercolours. In 1981 the Nautical College in Bristol, where he was teaching ship stability, closed and the decoy carving that had replaced the model ships in his spare time became a full time occupation. Ducks seemed a natural progression for him, the sea was still a part of him, and he greatly admired the navigational abilities of the wildfowl. Apart from making traditional and decorative decoys, he enjoyed teaching at his workshop near Bristol and seeing the growth of interest in decoys by both makers and collectors.

Sadly, Robert Ridges died during the preparation of this book.

Pair of mallards and a pair of scamps all fully feather textured and painted in acrylics.

Coat of Arms of the Duke of Norfolk in lime.

Coat of Arms of the Duke of Norfolk in lime, after painting and gilding in oil.

John Roberts

Born in South Wales, John Roberts gained a diploma in art and design at Gloucestershire College of Art in Cheltenham, followed by three years at the London Art School studying wood and stonecarving. The next ten years were spent as a stone carver, working on Westminster Abbey. He later took a teaching post at the City and Guild School in Kensington, which he retains to this day in a part time capacity.

Alongside his teaching, John has undertaken a wide variety of commissions in wood and stone, both restoration and some new work. Of late, he has found that he has been able to devote a greater portion of his time to more creative work and his first solo exhibition took place in 1989. This development now heads his future plans.

*Chinese-style occasional table in
Indian rosewood.*

Waring Robinson

Waring Robinson has been a doctor all his working life with a
love of wood that has developed with the passing of time, as
has his skill in cabinetmaking. Over the years he has entered
competitions and visited exhibitions, keeping abreast of
current design and techniques. Now retirement is on the
horizon and in preparation for this he is beginning to sell his
work, paving the way for his second career.

Edward Robinson

A triptych is chiefly used as an altar piece, and
although in the great Gothic cathedrals of
western Europe they were often of considerable
size, it is possible that the form was originally
conceived on a much smaller scale and designed
to be portable. This triptych entitled
Transfiguration V was carved in lavoa by Edward
Robinson ". . . a painter who has found, rather
late in life, that wood is the medium I should
have been working in all along."

*"Transfiguration V" in lavoa. The title refers to
the relationship between the inner and outer
designs. Each of the side panels has a similar
design both inside and outside. When closed, the
triptych gives the appearance of a misfit, or at
best an incomplete whole; when open these side
panels are seen to be part of, and necessary to, a
larger and more mysterious whole.*

Photographs courtesy of Michael Dudley.

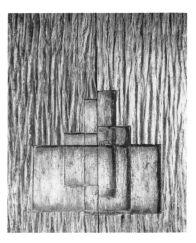

Desmond Ryan

"My aim has been, and will continue to be, to achieve the best possible solution to a problem, make it to the best of my ability in the shortest possible time — this has rarely, if ever, happened."
Desmond Ryan

Domino set. Box in padauk with brass inlay; dominoes in African blackwood with sycamore spots.

Frame with doors for limited edition print by Graham Clarke, burr elm veneer with boxwood inlay.

Dressing table in sycamore. (Closed)
Dressing table in sycamore. (Open)

139

Camelot chair in ash.

Macassar ebony collector's cabinet, awarded the Guild Mark from the Worshipful Company of Furniture Makers.

Lady's dressing table and matching stool in Honduras rosewood.

David Savage

David Savage has been a furniture maker and designer for twenty years. In the late sixties he gained a degree in fine art at Oxford and did a post graduate course at the Royal Academy School. Since then he has been establishing and expanding his own company in the ancient north Devon port of Bideford. He employs a small team, one of whom is training to assist him with the design work, an aspect of the business which makes increasing demands on his time. After any one of the many exhibitions at which the workshop is represented, David spends many hours at the drawing board following up enquiries and commissions, returning to the bench for the prototype and more specialised work.

Apart from the individual commissions, the workshop also makes a range of pieces, including the Camelot chair, which can be produced, when commissioned, as a small batch item, altering the detailing to the customer's preference.

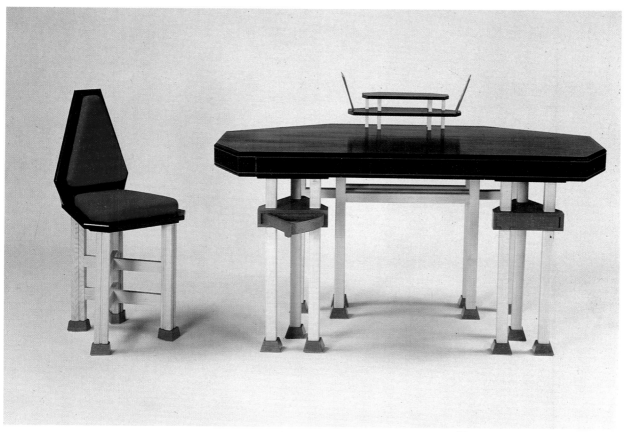

Photograph courtesy of Christies.

Oil rig desk.

Stephen Owen

This "Oil Rig Desk" and matching chair made by Stephen Owen were sold at auction by Christies to a private client. The top of the desk is black stained ash, the feet red stained veneer and the legs ash. Small cabinets in the front legs open to reveal drawers.

Stephen enjoys the bold era of change of the 1930's and his elephant table, made of bleached sycamore and elephant hide is another example of his own attempts to emulate this boldness. Following an art foundation course at Cardiff Art College, he went to the John Makepeace School for Craftsmen in Wood and has been designing and making furniture for the past nine years.

Elephant table. Bleached sycamore and elephant hide.

141

Sidetable. Thuya burr, silver,
tortoiseshell and satinwood legs.

Clock. Burr walnut and stirling silver.

Display case for silver salts, English
walnut, burr walnut, silver and suede.

Side table in Kingwood and silver.

142

Silver Lining Workshops

Mark Boddington trained as a silversmith before studying furniture making and design at Parnham House for two years. It was here that he met Adrian Foote, who was serving a five year apprenticeship in the John Makepeace workshops. In 1985, when they had completed their respective studies they established the Silver Lining Workshops in converted Victorian farm buildings on the estate of the Duke of Westminster at Aldford, Chester. The partners specialise in combining the precise skills of silversmithing with those of fine furniture making. Although brass, gold and silver can be seen in antiques, it is more unusual to see the precious metals worked into contemporary furniture. They envisage using increasingly more silver in their pieces.

"We are succeeding in rewarding the artisan/craftsman who traditionally has never been able to see the returns for his excellence in his own lifetime. Our continuing success will ensure that Silver Lining Workshops makes a significant contribution in the 1990's to the revival of decorative art. With the available number of good genuine antiques diminishing there is a growing market for the very best in craftsmanship, design and materials."

A silver hallmark registered at the London Assay Office serves as a signature on the work, which is bought and commissioned by both corporate and private clients, architects and interior designers.

Clock. Burr elm, with silver inlay and hands.

Garden seat in teak.

143

S.F. Furniture

Ian Hesletine and Declan O'Donahue met at the John Makepeace School for Craftsmen at Parnham House in Dorset. Ian began his two year stay in 1977 and immediately on his graduation started working for himself at Street Farm Workshops in Acton Turville. Declan joined him in 1980, and they have been working together ever since. Both have very similar aims and objectives, in that they set both short term and long term goals to work towards, seeking to get that little bit more from the next piece. Ian thinks some of his major achievements could be as far away as thirty years.

They compliment each other on the outside elements that they allow to influence their work: the honest approach of the Arts and Crafts Movement, making furniture for using rather than looking at; the rich colours of the Art Deco and Art Nouveau periods; and the importance of space in furniture, which they liken to the rest bars in music.

They have a mixed clientele comprising those commissioning domestic furniture; a small number of companies requiring boardroom and senior management furniture; and a few enquiries for short runs of smaller items. "The desire to produce larger numbers is there," Ian explained, "but not at the expense of quality, and I am not fooled by the statement that excellent furniture can be cheap. Fine quality furniture can never be cheap and, equally, does not need to be extortionately expensive."

Circular dining/conference table, designed and made by both partners. The top is solid English brown oak, the legs laminated brown oak. This piece was awarded a Guild Mark by the Worshipful Company of Furniture Makers.

144

Sectional conference table in American red oak designed and made by Ian Heseltine. Sectional conference table fully extended.

Range of office accessories in ebonised Brazilian mahogany and brass designed and made by both partners.

Games table shown with double pivoting boards, designed and made by Declan O'Donaghue. The top is in Indian rosewood, the legs are laminated rosewood. Chess board of Andaman paduak and satinwood. Backgammon board of Indian rosewood, Andaman paduak and satinwood; for cards, olive green gloving leather; and as a side table, consecutively laid oysters of laburnum.

Games table showing chess board only.

Jon Shaw

Jon Shaw has been designing and making furniture for ten years, exhibiting his work up and down the country. Prior to this, he took an honours degree in three dimensional design and worked as a cabinet maker for John Makepeace. Now he is happy to be able to pay the bills doing what he enjoys most, working to commission for a variety of clients from his own workshop near Badminton. He would like in the future to be able to employ a cabinet maker and spend more time designing and marketing his work, but until then he will continue to do all of these tasks himself, as well as teach part time at the Faculty of Art and Design, in Bower Aston, near Bristol.

Bookcase in padauk and wenge. Dining table in padauk and ebony.

Dining table in laminated burr elm with African walnut surround, four chairs and two carvers in African walnut with leather upholstery.

"Convertible" batch produced four-function table in natural and black ash, shown in two of the four positions: the low coffee table and the large dining table. The top and frame are interconnected by a patented pivot device making conversion from one position to the next very easy.

Lee Sinclair

"The major influence on my work must be the craft revival that has taken place since the early '70's which has given me the patronage and thus the freedom to experiment with new forms and shapes. My disillusionment with the British furniture industry, where the salesman determines the design policy, made me realise that the only way to produce new innovative designs was for a designer to manage, design, manufacture and make his own work. This has been the principle behind our workshop where we specialise in commissioned work but also produce batch made items for a wider clientele."
Lee Sinclair

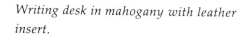

Writing desk in mahogany with leather insert.

147

Michael Norris

Michael Norris has been a furniture maker and designer for the last fourteen years, teaching part time at the Medway College of Art and Design. His interest in wood began as a small boy and he remembers nostalgically living next door to Sam Rockall, the last true chair bodger of the Chiltern Hills, and later living amongst wooden boat builders on the East Coast. Michael works with other craftsmen from the Star Brewery Workshop in Lewes, Sussex.

Elm table.

Detail of pinned joints in rail.

*Elm burr
"Archaeological"
series.*

Photograph courtesy Hugo Barclay.

Mike Scott

Born and educated in England, Mike Scott emigrated to Australia, where he
spent ten years working as an accountant and administrator. On his return in
1982 he attended Crewe and Alsager College gaining a degree in Creative Arts. It
was at college that he was first introduced to the lathe and in 1984 with the aid
of the Enterprise Allowance Scheme he began working for himself as a
woodturner.

". . . I try to create pieces which have 'presence', it may be a feeling of antiquity
— or a stunning grain pattern, a sensual shape or a monumental form. I don't
work to any formula — each piece is individual and intuitively evolved in the
process of making."

*Elm burr
bowl.*

*Jarah burr
bowl.*   Photographs courtesy of Ron Solman.

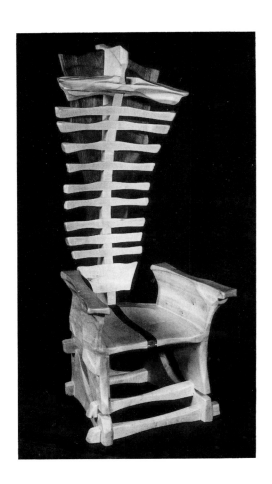

Tim Stead

Tim Stead is a furniture designer, maker and sculptor with a passion for wood and trees. It is his driving force — so much so that in 1986 he made and sold 365 wooden axe heads, one for every day of the year, raising £3,500 to help buy a piece of woodland for the community. From this small beginning, Tim and two colleagues eventually raised £30,000 to buy 30 acres, ripe for woodland management and replanting. The project is on-going, and it is the group's aim that the site be used educationally as well as for conservation. Woodland activities, such as chair bodging, will also be encouraged. Tim finds the project very exciting and enjoys being able to go there and consider the management and ecological aspects, hoping that it will inspire others to do similar things.

Chair in walnut and sycamore.

Oak table on tressle base. Four standing chairs, two elm, one ash and one oak. Corset chair, mahogany, so called because of the lacing at the back.

Chest of drawers in ash.

Paul Spriggs

Paul Spriggs' ambition is to build a pipe organ, but in the meantime he makes rush seated chairs in the style of Ernest Gimson, and other complimentary items of furniture. Paul was trained as an architect and made the transition to chair maker eight years ago when he set up his workshop in Cirencester in the Cotswolds.

Slat-back rocking chair in ash with rushed seat.

Philip St Pier

Trained at the John Makepeace School for Craftsmen in Wood, Parnham, from 1977 to 1979, Philip St Pier joined two other colleagues at Street Farm Workshop, Acton Turville. Apart from a small range of pieces, including this consort desk which are made to order and numbered, Philip also carries out commissions for private and corporate clients.

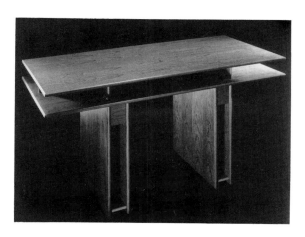

Perennial garden seat in iroko.

Consort desk in American cherry.

151

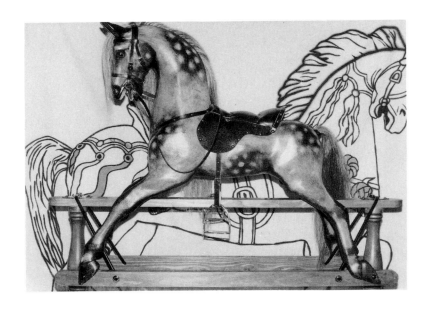

Marc and Tony Stevenson

Twins, Marc and Tony Stevenson started Stevenson Brothers seven years ago, near Ashford in Kent. The making of rocking horses has been in the family for over forty-five years, Tony learnt the trade by serving an apprenticeship with Uncle James Bosworthick, while Marc was studying for his degree in graphic design at Bristol. They make and restore rocking horses of all descriptions and recently achieved one of their ambitions, making a carousel. It was a hand cranked juvenile carousel of twelve horses and two carriages commissioned through Harrods. They both enjoy their work and the pleasure that it brings to small children. For Tony and Marc, rocking horses are not just work, they are a science, and they mean to be its foremost authority.

A selection of rocking horses from the Stephenson Brothers stable.

Preening Grebe.

Oystercatcher.

Guy Taplin

Guy Taplin's interest in birds originated about 14 years ago when he was working in Regents Park looking after the birds on the island. His workshop is on the beach at Wivenhoe, Essex, where he has access to driftwood and reclaimed timber, although he frequently has to laminate pieces to achieve the sizes he needs.

He originally started by selling his work through antique shops but now most of his work is sold at exhibitions and galleries.

Shelduck.

Bowl of Jarrah root.

Jules Tattersall

"The use of a particular type of material, namely grass tree root, helped me to see the possibilities with textured finishes due to its remarkable grain structure being fairly soft. It also allowed me to develop the hollow pot form that I enjoy so much. I am now taking these textures and forms into other timbers and larger pieces. Whilst I recognise the importance of originality of design, I am more and more drawn towards simple traditional bowl forms as these are the most satisfying to me." Jules Tattersall

Hollow pot in oak.

Hollow pot in grass tree root.

154

Chris Stott

Based in Scunthorpe, woodturner Chris Stott encourages others by teaching part time at the Humberside Adult Education Centre and demonstrating at exhibitions and shows. He is now doing more experimental work, developing his technique further and increasing his range of turned items.

Natural edged bowl in burr elm.

Ian Taylor

The furniture course at Shrewsbury College was just the beginning for Ian Taylor, and since leaving there three years ago he has continued the learning process of matching the creative side of the work to the technical. For this process of discovery he has set himself some restrictions: he does not use applied decoration, colour, man-made boards or lacquers, feeling that ". . . solid wood is enough of a challenge."

Box on stand in sugar maple. The box lifts off the stand and has three sliding trays just below the lid.

Photographs courtesy of Hector Innes.

155

Zachary Taylor

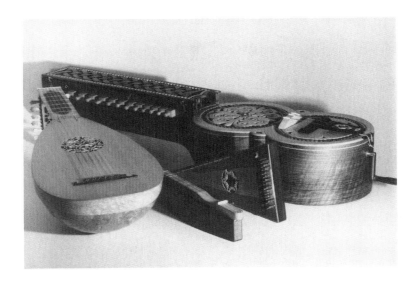

This organistrum in walnut, made by Zachary, is an early hurdy gurdy, the original of which forms part of the sculptured entrance to the shrine of St James the Apostle at Santiago de Compostela. The research to discover as yet unseen early musical instruments is the largest and most fascinating part of Zach's work. He studies mediaeval manuscripts, icons, pew ends, stained glass windows and sculptures, reproducing the pieces faithfully in known traditional methods and timbers.

Not content with discovering and making the pieces, Zachary directs the Rozata Consort of Ancient Music, a group of costumed musicians, who perform on such instruments. The psaltery in sequoia and rosewood, the Apalachian dulcimer and the lute in bird's-eye maple with ebony and rosewood trim complete the quartet of instruments illustrated here.

A pair of butter-spoons in cherry.

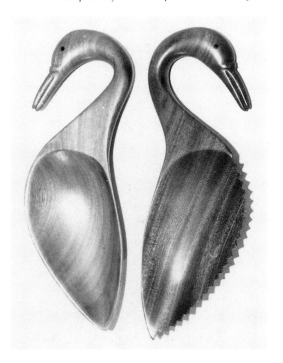

Malcolm Thomas

Anniversary lovespoon in cherry.

Malcolm Thomas is a traditional Welsh spoon carver, taught by his late grandfather. Recognition as a spoon carver takes second place to Malcolm's prime objective, which is to ensure the continuation of the family's tradition in the art of spoon carving, where all spoons such as tea-spoons, broth-spoons, butter-spoons, ladles and lovespoons are hand carved by traditional methods from native woods to reveal the flower grain centrally in each spoon bowl, as in this lovespoon commemorating a 25th wedding anniversary, "Rwy'n dy Garu — I love you".

Brian Tomnay

The sections of this desk, by Brian Tomnay, are seen to hang together in fragmented form reminiscent of the exfoliation of granite, the breaking up of the rock due to weathering, and the colours used are muted green, grey and a grey tinted blue to reflect the Scottish landscape. Brian has collected many accolades on his way through both Rycotewood College and Glasgow School of Art. It is his intention to start a Glasgow based small batch production workshop producing furniture of a Scottish aspect.

Desk in sycamore.

Frank Triggs

"I love ideas; ways of looking at and learning about the world. I have studied the development of perception in children and have made toys and educational aids for those with learning difficulties. I am fascinated by the world views of other cultures and how these are reflected in their artefacts and architecture. I make images to visualise ideas. In recent years woodcarving has become the core of my activity.
At the same time I've become more concerned with ideas about ecology and technologies that work with Nature rather than against it." Frank Triggs

Photographs courtesy of Peter Griffiths.

Crow, 1.8m (6ft) wing-span. The body is carved in relief, sandblasted and then recarved, before staining and polishing. Flowers, foliage and eyes are individually turned and carved and assembled on sprung stems. Lime, sycamore, elm, yew, holly, robinia and padauk. Courtesy of Mr and Mrs D. Jenks.

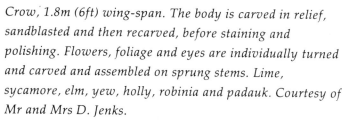

"Spot of bother"

"Flapper girl."

Alan Townsend

Alan Townsend is a self-taught marquetarian, who has worked with wood as long as he can remember. In the last four years he has won the Marquetry Society's Rosebowl award three times.

"Our mutual friend."

"Siberian reflection."

Carved box, basswood.

Carved box, iroko.

Still life, Quebec pine.

Howard Raybould

Howard Raybould studied sculpture at Ravensbourne College of Art, and the techniques of woodcarving at an architectural woodcarver's workshop in London. He has worked for over twelve years using both disciplines to achieve ''. . . a richness of surface combined with an informal sense of theatre.'' Travelling plays an important part in the development of his work, especially his time spent in Japan where he became fascinated by their wood block prints on textiles. He pursues his own relaxed style of woodcarving and some of his more recent ideas are colourful wall panels made of assembled shapes of plywood, shallowly carved. Howard sells his work through contemporary art galleries, craft galleries and exhibitions.

Robin Wardle

The inspiration for many of Robin Wardle's pieces comes from a variety of sources: seed heads, shells, fragments of anatomy, pond organisms, strange fruit and vegetables. Emphasis is placed on the idea of hollow objects which are intended as containers. They are made from complex constructions, fabricated from flat pieces of carefully matched wood and then carved, shaped and finished to explore the latent and unique quality of the material.

Vessel with lid, oak, blue stained with iron sulphate hand marbled paper lining.

Vessel, wenge.

Photographs courtesy of John Coles

Lidded vessel, wenge, brazilian rosewood hinge tulipwood peg, silver pin.

159

Original design horse in canter position in mahogany.

Traditional dapple grey rocking horse

Harold Wakefield

This traditional dapple grey was carved by Harold Wakefield, who has now been carving rocking horses for thirty years. He was apprenticed to a local village wheelwright and carpenter and this included learning a wide variety of skills including making farm carts and gates, churchwork, signwriting and gilding, graining, marbling and french polishing. Also, as with all village wheelwrights at the time, they undertook the profession of undertaker.

Harold works from his home at Boston in Lincolnshire and strives to break away from the traditionally accepted positions of rocking horses. He has designed this mahogany horse in a canter pose.

Cabinet in fumed and white waxed oak, with stainless steel details, maple interior. Designed to occupy a bricked up inglenook in a 16th century farmhouse.

Storage and display column in wenge, rippled ash and ivory.

Sine Screen: lacquered plywood held in tension on stainless steel rods, ash uprights.

Photographs courtesy of Walter Gardiner.

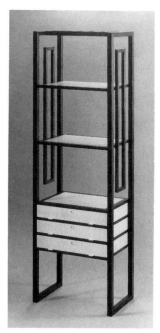

Rod Wales

"I first set up my workshop in 1981. Since then much of my work has been commissioned, one-off furniture, often for private customers, though in the last few years the number of business clients has increased dramatically. There have been occasional fruitful collaborations with architects and interior designers. Alongside the commissioned work we have designed and are currently manufacturing two ranges of products in small batches. I work primarily with wood, incorporating metal, glass, plastic, stone, etc. While I believe summaries are only of limited value (by definition), leaving many questions unanswered, I would say of my own work that I am concerned with the controlled but vigorous expression of materials, structure and workmanship to produce objects that have vitality and which outlast the flavour of the month. I do not mean to suggest that I am, or wish to be, ignorant of fashion; I recognise the potency, both commercial and aesthetic of some flavours, but try to take a longer view." Rod Wales

"Button Down" plywood waste paper bins and desk tidys.

Folding chair in ash with natural hide seat.

Reclining chair and foot stool; these are both adjustable and folding. Made of steam bent ash, the structure is light, strong and flexible, adjusting to any unevenness in the floor. Upholstered and rattan.

162

Photographs courtesy of Neil Badger.

Stacking chairs with upholstered and plywood seats.

Upholstered reclining chair and foot stool in ash.

Rattan reclining chair and foot stool in ash.

Trannon Furniture Makers

When David Colwell graduated from the Royal College of Art he worked initially as a designer in London, moving to Wales twelve years ago to an old schoolhouse where he now lives and works. He makes tables and predominantly steam bent chairs to his own design in small production runs. For most of his work he uses local, fast growing ash for its strength and suitability, choosing it still standing, or recently felled.

The criteria David works to is a demanding one: he wants to create a visual expression, an image of, or an approach to, manufacture that is appropriate to today and the future, having a low impact on the environment, preferably for the better. He looks to low capital investment, with rewarding and profitable employment; and his furniture must be useful, and stand the test of time.

His future objective is to develop his present work into the commercial mainstream without compromise, and then, perhaps, to begin experimenting with another medium.

Tables and chairs in contract use at Blakes Head Restaurant, York.

Photograph courtesy of Richard Singleton.

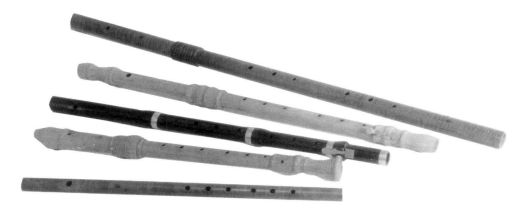

Sycamore bass Renaissance flute.

Boxwood Baroque flute.

Ebony and silver Baroque flute.

Boxwood alto recorder — copy of Denver's original in ivory in the Royal College of Music museum.

Pear alto Renaissance flute.

John Underhill

John Underhill has been making reproductions of Renaissance and Baroque musical instruments for the last nine years. At present he is concentrating on flutes. He studies the instruments and drawings in museums before making them, ensuring that the new instrument is as close to the original as possible whilst taking into account the requirements of present day musicians.

Clavichords by David Weldon.

David Weldon

The clavichord was the favourite instrument of many Renaissance and Baroque composers, most notably the Bach family. David Weldon is making instruments which he hopes meets the standards they would have required then, but within a simpler carcase for today's modern decor. He trained at the music technology department of the London College of Furniture, and now returns as a part time lecturer to ensure continuity of the art.

Low table in elm.

Waywood

Rad Segrt and Barnaby Scott work together from a small workshop in Oxfordshire, designing and making all types of furniture, mainly in temperate hardwoods. Essential to all working partnerships is the ability to combine and complement one another's skills. Rad is the main designer, the source of many of his ideas being natural forms. Tree roots, for example, would appear to be behind the design for this low table in elm. Barnaby is the more practical of the two and he sees himself principally as a craftsman, converting Rad's designs into reality.

Sculptured chest in elm with oak hinges.

Small chest in burr elm.

Matching sideboard in English walnut.

Dining table and chairs English walnut. The client requested an Art Nouveau style.

Photographs courtesy of Stop by Stop

Andrew Varah

"Having lived and worked abroad for twelve years architecture has been my major influence. Each culture has influenced a theme or detail I wished to explore. Now, having four very talented cabinet makers working for me, including Andrew Whateley, I wish my workshop to produce pieces which really are superb examples of furniture. The cost must be such that any prospective client must feel he has excellent value and that no-one could better our craftsmanship. My pieces must stand the test of time and be appreciated in the next century and thereafter. I should like to be known for executing very complex commissions, and perhaps for the fact that in many pieces I build a secret compartment, giving the client twelve months to find what has been hidden, before I retrieve the hidden object and reveal the secret opening." Andrew Varah

166

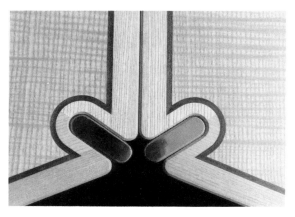

Detail of modular conference table.

Modular conference table in fiddle back ash and walnut.

Two of a set of dining chairs in oak.

Photographs courtesy of Paul Lapsley.

Seating for Sir Christopher Wren's city church of St Stephen, Walbrook, in German white beech. The commission was to design seating that would compliment the only altar Henry Moore sculpted.

Photographs courtesy of Stop by Stop.

Detail of church seating.

Low table in sycamore and ebony.

Photographs courtesy of Keith James.

Ewan Welsh

In the three years since he left the John Makepeace School for Craftsmen at Parnham, Ewan Welsh has set out determinedly to make furniture making his career. Working from Halifax, Ewan accepts commissions for both corporate and private clients, as well as producing a range of small batch items, including this low table that can be bought at various retail outlets in London, Manchester and Leeds.

"Aspects of the Coast", chestnut root.

David West

David West attended the Camberwell School of Art from 1958 to 1960 and is primarily an artist, whose use of wood has developed from his painting. *Aspects of the Coast*, carved in chestnut root, is one of a series of twelve pieces which have evolved from his walks along the Dorset coastline, near his home in Lyme Regis.

168

Shell box in solid fiddleback sycamore.

Andrew Whateley

Andrew Whateley has recently started working with Andrew Varah in Warwickshire. Until then he had worked as an interpretative craftsman making other people's furniture since 1969, first for John Makepeace and then at the Royal College of Art. The eleven years he spent with Makepeace (the first five as an apprentice), influenced him greatly, the Royal College less so, although it presented the opportunity for him to start designing for himself. It was here that a student created the technical challenge of bending and twisting solid wood to form chair backs. Andrew later worked on this technique to produce a prototype chair using various bending and twisting techniques. These ideas won him the Worshipful Company of Furniture Makers' Designer Craftsman Award to investigate inventive woodbending techniques. This pair of steam bent chairs of solid quarter-sawn English oak are the result, the arms and front leg are bent in one piece and connected with brass verdigris fittings; the finish is textured, created by using caustic soda and ammonia.

Pair of steam bent chairs in quarter-sawn English oak.

Photograph courtesy of Frank Thurston.

David and Jean Whitaker

David and Jean Whitaker are a husband and wife team working from Ickleton in Essex. Their designs are based on earlier British furniture makers such as Barnsley, Gimson and Mackintosh. They would like to see their furniture in everyday use, becoming a family possession that is passed from father to son for generations to come.

Writing desk in American cherry.

Peter White

Marquetarian Peter White teaches his skills to the local Meopham marquetry club encouraging the increasing interest in the craft. He has won numerous awards of the Marquetry Society of Great Britain. *Tawny at the Wheel* won first prize at the recent London Woodworker Exhibition, and was used to decorate the front cover of *The Marquetry Manual*.

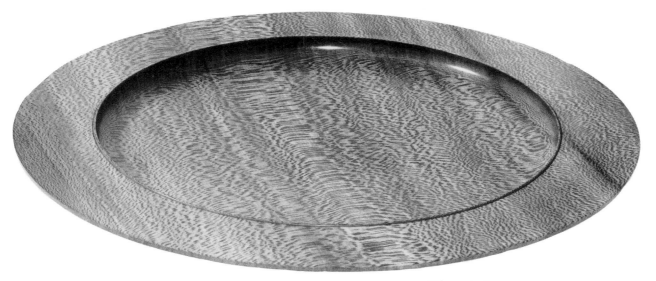

Platter in lacewood, 17½'' diameter.

Don White

For Don White, woodturning in some way or other occupies his thoughts and actions for most of his waking hours. It is a total commitment. Apart from his creative work, he accepts regular orders for domestic bowls and platters believing that there is no substitute for the discipline of repetition work to give the hand, eye and brain the co-ordination so necessary when attempting to create balanced individual pieces. Don has been turning now for twelve years and providing for his family is his main objective; the fact that he is able to accomplish this doing something he enjoys is a bonus.

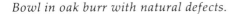

Bowl in oak burr with natural defects.

Bowl in silver gimlet burr, textured and scorched rim.

Bowl in spalted beech.

171

*Drinks trolley, sycamore, black
ash, black laminate and rubber.*

Whitehouse Workshops

"We are meticulous to ensure
that all the furniture we design
and make illustrates both our
design skill and the highest
standards of workmanship. It
is because of this that we
continue to be given the
opportunity of working on
increasingly challenging and
diverse projects. We seek to
increase the current interest in
furniture design and
encourage more people to
seriously consider
commissioning an
individually designed piece of
furniture." Rupert Senior and
Charles Wheeler Carmichael

Mechanical pool table.

Writing desk in wenge.

Photograph courtesy of Tim Imrie.

Antelope table, fumed acacia and ebony with removable legs and footrail.

Photograph courtesy of Keith Harding.

173

*Laminated walnut chair with
leather cushion and walnut desk
with silver inlay.*

Robin Williams

The source of Robin Williams' inspiration is evident in his designs, a love of water and the countryside. The organic forms so predominant in his furniture are largely derived from the material itself. Robin began working with wood as a child and after spending two years at the John Makepeace School for Craftsmen in Wood he set up his own workshop. He has recently moved to Harberton in Devon, where he employs a small team making individual commissions. Alongside this work he has also designed and made a rocking chair for small batch production in the same distinctive style.

Photographs courtesy of T. Grevatt.

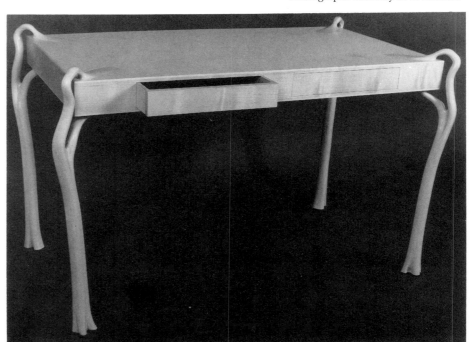

Sycamore writing desk.

Peter Wilder

This set of four tables, made in walnut, is one example of the reproduction style of Peter Wilder. He has now been making furniture for over thirty years, initially for a family furniture business in Downley, the last twenty years for himself. Peter enjoys the one-to-one relationship between a craftsman and his clients. Occasionally he exhibits his work, but most of the commissions originate by recommendation.

Set of four tables English walnut; the tops are quartered French burr walnut with herringbone inlay and cross banding.

Ferelyth Wills

Ferelyth Wills studied under John Skeaping at the Central School of Arts and Crafts in London, and has been a woodsculptor now for over fifty years. Even after all these years Ferelyth still feels that she has to make ". . . a good piece of sculpture; one that will be a truly three dimensional shape, which has the life and character of the subject, and which displays and is in keeping with, the natural beauty of the material."

Photographs courtesy of S.B. Wills.

"Skater" in yew.

Ebony figure (20" high)

"Mediaeval scene."

Eric Williamson

Fifteen years ago Eric Williamson began to carve rocking horses, using the offcuts to make marionettes. Up until this time he had tried his hand at teaching, furniture restoration and building. When he had built the workshop attached to his house in Powys, he discovered that the logistics of delivering rocking horses from Wales, combined with the problems of tangled string on the puppets was too much for him. He began making stringless marionettes, or automata, and has been doing so for twelve years, thus solving two problems at a stroke. As well as his character pieces which he makes in limited editions, Eric has made bigger pieces, namely a kinetic feature for one of the many modern shopping centres. The theme was a mediaeval village street scene, with much humorous activity taking place on the hour. He is employed at the moment on a "Mad Hatter's Tea Party" for a new gallery of automata in York. Eric's work is sold all over the world and he has recently returned from a promotional trip to Japan.

"Potter."

"Joiner."

"Mad Hatter's Teaparty."

Toby Winteringham

Having secured a degree in three dimensional design at Kingston Polytechnic, Toby Winteringham went on to get his Masters degree at the Royal College of Art. He began making furniture in 1978 and now produces small batch runs of furniture to generate business in the specialist retail markets. Commissions from architects and interior designers are actively sought. He sees future work expanding these ideas, but not beyond the point where personal control is lost, and he feels that a hands-on relationship with the work is vital to the maintenance of freshness and quality.

Marlin, eclipse low table. The top is solid English cherry supported on a blue stained laminated curved slab and a black stained spike leg. The spot is inlaid black veneer.

Square chair and table. Part of a range of lightweight dining furniture in plain and ebonised beech.

177

Canterbury Tales.

Chaucer. (From Canterbury Tales series.)

Tim and Vicki Wood

After gaining a degree in mechanical engineering Tim Wood trained as a cabinet maker under Edward Baly, the founder of the Devon Guild. His wife, Vicki, was a potter with a lifelong interest in old boats. Seven years ago they joined forces to make and sell automata. They take their inspiration from historical themes coupled with their own imagination to give their pieces humour and movement. The mechanisms can be hand turned, motor driven or worked by a pull cord. To date their work has been sold in America, Japan, Germany and Switzerland as well as here at home. Perhaps one of the most interesting commissions to date was for five large motor driven pieces, depicting the liner Canberra, which are being used for publicity purposes by the P & O shipping line. Tim and Vicki enjoy their work and the pleasure and amusement that their automata give to those who see them.

178

Knight and
Lion.

Brittania.

Provident. (From the Miniature Maritime series.)

Farmer and Bull.

179

Michael Wood

At the age of eight Michael Wood's artistic ability became apparent when he was in Canada with his family and began to paint the abundant wild life. The interest has never left him, and now Michael carves his birds in three dimensions rather than paint them in two. Having no formal training, it is his love of birds which has encouraged him to research his subject and train himself in the techniques of his craft.

Pintail Drake.

David Woodward

When woodturner, David Woodward is not at his lathe he is out in the countryside felling trees for local landowners. In this way he is able to tell his clients exactly where the wood came from, why it was cut down and in some instances produce a photograph of the standing tree. There will never be any shortage of raw materials for David as he lives in a beautifully wooded part of Brecon in South Wales, and replants trees as often as is possible.

Six platters in lacewood.

John Wyndham

John Wyndham eventually succumbed to the rigours of being a full time craftsman and last year took a part time indefinite sabbatical. His workshop made a variety of furniture to commission, both architectural and domestic, as well as a range of garden furniture in small batch runs. John still carries out commissions, but without the same pressures, and is learning to enjoy designing and making again. The double doors shown here were undertaken for a client who had worked on a film in which the beech tree featured. Although the tree was heavily scarred by a chainsaw it was to be used, for sentimental reasons, for his photographic studio. The cuts, which pierce the door, are filled with a clear blue resin letting through a shaft of blue light when the sun shines.

Double doors in beech.

Knock down, king-sized bed in sycamore and fumed acacia.

Photographs courtesy of Walter Gardiner.

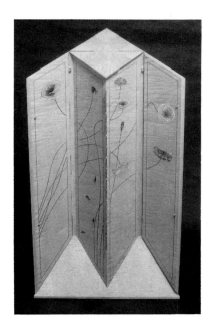
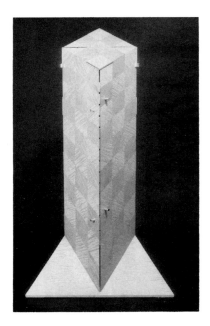
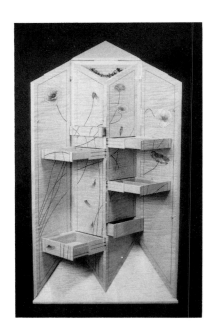

Jewellery chest in figured sycamore with inland stems. Enamelled flowers by Jane Short.

Rupert Williamson

After studying for his Diploma in art and design at Wycombe College, Rupert Williamson attended the Royal College of Art for his Masters degree. He now returns to various colleges as a visiting lecturer of three dimensional design. London was the first home for his workshop, but after a year he moved to his present address in Milton Keynes where he works with his two assistants. He regards himself as a sculptor, using furniture as a medium in which to express his work, and within the scope of his customers' requirements, follows this course. Using mainly contrasting woods, he employs lines to define form, to show the interplay between structure and decoration and to emphasise sculptural qualities.

Chair in ebony and figured sycamore.

Library table in hornbeam.

Armchair in satinwood.

*Decorative shelves in Macassar ebony
and sycamore.*

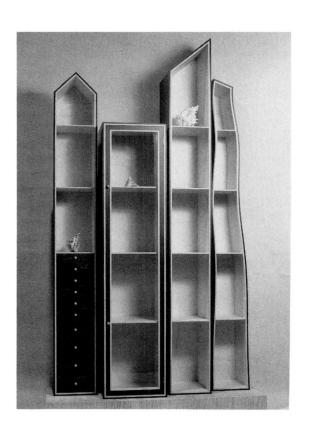

John Wilsher

"... I enjoy the challenge of making a copy of an original piece of furniture as made by one of the great masters."

John Wilsher

The Carlton House desk is semi-circular in plan, veneered in Rio rosewood with satinwood crossbanding. The legs are turned, the tope twist at the top of the leg is carved, the reeds are also cut by hand. The two Sphinx heads are of brass and set into the legs. The centre section is hinged to afford a writing and reading slope, under which a well is situated. The three large drawers are bordered by a brass bead against a rosewood edging, two secret drawers are hidden within a compartment.

The sofa table is an exact measured copy of one by Chippendale the Younger. The original can be seen at Stourhead House in Wiltshire. Veneered in Rio rosewood with satinwood crossbanding with boxwood and rosewood inlay. The lyre ends and stretcher rail are carved, the splayed legs are reeded.

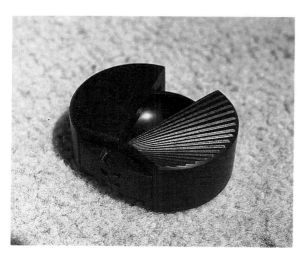

Miniature profile box in ebony with hinge and tray.

Box in burr elm and ebony with boxwood pegs and silk thread.

Box in yew with silk thread.

Richard Windley

Richard Windley has been making his boxes for twelve years. They are made in all shapes, sizes, and timbers using a wide range of techniques. This combination added to his own design ability ensures a tremendous variety in his products. Most of the boxes are small and will fit comfortably in the hand, but larger boxes have been undertaken for dressing tables and desks. Richard feels that his interest in Art Deco design and in the Japanese attitude to craftsmanship may be perceptible in his current work. He spends some of his time teaching small studio practice at the Hereford College of Art and Design when not working at his home near Ludlow in Shropshire.

Box in ebony and robinia with silk thread.

Box in burr elm and kingwood with an ebony hinge.

Brian Winter

Caithness is one of the northern-most counties of the British Isles and home of furniture maker and designer Brian Winter. He started his career with a seven year apprenticeship followed by one year as a journeyman. That was over forty years ago, now he works and teaches at his workshop in Lyth, producing such pieces as this Norse chair in ash, which harks back to the Viking legacy of the Highlands and displays the influence of the Scottish architect and designer Charles Rennie Mackintosh.

Norse chair in ash.

Photograph courtesy of Aviemore Photographic.

John Wright

The Little Angel Theatre in Islington, North London, has become a place of pilgrimage for visiting puppeteers from all over the world. It was started by puppet maker John Wright in 1960. He has been making puppets since 1938, when, seeing a performance of Podrecca's *Piccoli* he was motivated to learn more about them, how they were carved and about the theatres. John has been the standard bearer in winning for the puppet theatre a place of critical esteem as an authentic form of contemporary art.

Carved puppet.

Index of Names

Andrew Alcock
The Workshops
1 Beehive Lane
Chelmsford
Essex CM2 9SU

Nick Allen
Ground Floor Studio
80b Battersea Rise
London SW11 1EH

John Ambrose
12 Silver Street
Ely
Cambridgeshire CB7 4JF

John Anderson
20 Silvergate
Blickling
Norwich
Norfolk NR11 6NN

Freddie Baier
1a Church Street
Pewsey
Wiltshire SN9 5DL

David Bailey
21 Downing Avenue
May Bank
Newcastle under Lyme
Staffordshire ST5 0JY

Peter Bailey
Cnocan
Camus Croise
Isle Ornsay
Isle of Skye IV43 8QS

John Baldwin
52 Purley Park Road
Purley
Surrey CR2 2BS

Chris Barney
Brook Farm
Birdingbury
Rugby
Warwickshire CV23 8EN

Robert Beal
Commercial Mill
Savile Street
Milnsbridge
Huddersfield
Yorkshire HD3 4PG

Hugh Birkett
Mitford Oak House

Church Street
Moreton in Marsh
Gloucestershire GL56 0LN

Richard Blizzard
Five Leaves
Bussage
Stroud
Gloucestershire GL6 0LN

Mark Boddington
See Silver Lining Workshops

David Bowerman
Godlingston Manor Workshops
Swanage
Dorset BH19 3DJ

Kenneth Bowers
Wayfarers
Victoria Road
Saltburn-by-the-Sea
Cleveland TS12 1JD

Chris Briggs
Woodknot Crafts
Fullbridge Wharf
Maldon
Essex CM9 7QH

Jeremy Broun
1 Frankley Terrace
Bath
Avon BA1 6DP

Anthony Bryant
The Loft
Breageside
Porthleven
Helston
Cornwall TR13 9JU

Fraser Budd
73 Roman Way
Stoke Bishop
Bristol
Avon BS9 1SP

Jean Burhouse
The Old Sawmill
Inver
Dunkeld
Perthshire PH8 0JR

Lee Burman
See Kingswood & Burman

Matthew Burt
Albany Cottages
Sherrington

Warminster
Wiltshire BA12 0SP

Ashley Cartwright
Elizabeth House
Weedon Lois
Towcester
Northamptonshire NN12 1LZ

Paul Caton
Wellspring Cottage
Deerfold
Lingen
Bucknell
Shropshire SY7 0EE

Cerdan Limited
Silver Street Workshop
37a Silver Street
Ashwell
Baldock
Hertfordshire SG7 5QH

Philip Chambers
31 Quarry Park Road
Cheam
Sutton
Surrey SM1 2DR

Chameleon Interior Furnishing
Flat 2
96 Birch Lane
Rusholme
Manchester M13 0WW

Samuel Chan
2 Pentland Gardens
Wandsworth
London SW18 2AN

Jess Christman
Grieves Cottage
Snawdon Farm
Gifford
East Lothian EH41 4PJ

Neil Clarke
High Croft
Chapel Lane
Kniveton
Ashbourne
Derbyshire DE6 1JP

Brian Cohen
Rosedene
Peaslake Lane
Peaslake
Guildford
Surrey GU5 9RJ

David Colwell
See Trannon Furniture Makers

Eric Cooper
16 Glebe Road
Barnes
London SW13 0EA

Max Cooper
Moss Workshops
Moss House Farm
Yarnfield
Stone
Staffordshire ST15 0NF

Stephen Cooper
28 Trooper Road
Aldbury
Tring
Hertfordshire HP23 5RW

Jeremy Cornwell
4 Albert Park Road
Malvern
Worcestershire WR14 1HN

Andrew Crawford
Unit B02
Acton Business Centre
School Road
London NW10 6TD

Benedict Critchley
Patmore Lodge
Albury
Ware
Hertfordshire SG11 2LT

Helen Cumberlidge
See Cumberlidge & Jenkinson

Cumberlidge & Jenkinson
The Wood Studio
The Old Postern
Dartington
Totnes
Devon TQ9 6EA

Roger Curry
Dinham Cottage, Dinham
Ludlow
Shropshire SY8 1EJ

Huw Davies
See Kodama

Detail
D2 Metropolitan Wharf
Wapping Wall
London E1 9SS

Philip Dobbins
Church Farm
Henshaw
Yeadon

Leeds
Yorkshire LS19 7SQ

Brian Dollemore
Birchmore Cottage
Nairwood Lane
Prestwood
Great Missenden
Buckinghamshire HP16 0QQ

Stephen Down
Shelly Farm Workshop
Morpeth
Northumberland NE61 4LP

Chris Dunseath
The Priory
Hinton St George
Somerset TA17 8SE

Nicholas Dyson
2 Home Farm
Ardington
Wantage
Oxfordshire OX12 8PN

Frank Egerton
94 Appley Lane
Appley Bridge
Wigan
Lancashire WN6 9AQ

Hugo Egleston
See Lasham Furniture Workshop

Marvin Elliott
Quindrie House
Hoxa
South Ronaldsay
Orkney
Scotland KW17 2TW

Robert Ellwood
Holroyd Mill
Beck Road
Micklethwaite
Bingley
West Yorkshire BD16 3JN

Alan Englefield
Owl Cottage
High Street
Netheravon
Salisbury
Wiltshire SP4 9PJ

F.B. Design
14 Hazel Road
Four Marks
Alton
Hampshire GU34 5EY

Sean Feeney
The Old School
Preston-on-Stour

Stratford-on-Avon
Warwickshire CV37 8NG

David Field
1b Marlborough Estate
159 Mortlake Road
Kew
Surrey TW9 4AW

Stephen Field
Cil-y-Byddar
Llambister Road
Llandrindod Wells
Powys LD1 5UW

Malcolm Fielding
2 Northern Terrace
Moss Lane
Silverdale
Carnforth
Lancashire LA5 0ST

Paul Fischer
West End Studio
West End
Chipping Norton
Oxfordshire OX7 5EY

Adrian Foote
See Silver Lining Workshops

David Forrest
See F.B. Design

Richard Foxcroft
2 Sunnyside
Wood End
Ardeley
Stevenage
Hertfordshire SG2 7BA

Martin Fraser
14 Pentre Isaf
Old Colwyn
Clwyd LL29 8UT

Dennis French
Rock House
Brimscombe Hill
Stroud
Gloucestershire GL5 2Q.R

Adam Gallimore
60 Greenhayes
Okeford Fitzpaine
Blandford Forum
Dorset DT11 0RE

Alan Glennie
92 Side Ley
Kegworth
Derbyshire DE7 2FJ

Geoff Godschalk
See Cerdan Limited

Raymond Gonzalez
Chardleigh House
Chardleigh Green
Wadeford
Chard
Somerset TA20 3AJ

Charles Good
23 Hamilton Way
Finchley
London N3 1AN

Neville Graydon
See Graydon Designs

Graydon Designs
7 Tomo Business Park
Creeting Road
Stowmarket
Suffolk IP14 5AY

David Gregson
Bridge Green Farm
Gissing Road
Burston
Diss
Norfolk IP22 3UD

Martin Greshoff
108a Caithness Road
Mitcham
Surrey CR4 2EW

Martin Grierson
22 Canham Road
London W3 7SR

Stephen Hallam
119–123 Sandycombe Road
Richmond
Surrey TW9 2ER

Ralph Hampton
101 Wilmot Street
Derby DE1 2JJ

Ian Harris
3 Cambridge Road
Wallasey
Wirral
Merseysire L45 1JF

Jonathan Hawkes
See Professional Woodworkers
Limited

Nansi Hemming
Bwlch Gwynt
Llanfair Road
Lampeter
Dyfed SA48 8JY

Michael Henderson
10 St Margaret's Place
Bradford-on-Avon
Wiltshire BA15 1DT

Ian Heseltine
See S.F. Furniture

Jeremy Higson
7 Hampton House
Industrial Estate
Hampton
Evesham
Worcestershire WR11 6PR

Jack Hill
PO Box 20
Midhurst
West Sussex GU29 0JD

Suzanne Hodgson
1 Banbury Road
Brackley
Northamptonshire NN13 6BB

Stephen Hounslow
See Pearl Dot Limited

Luke Hughes
1 Stukely Street
Covent Garden
London WC2B 5LQ

Mark Hutchins
12 Horsebridge Road
Westleigh
Havant
Hampshire PO9 2LH

Rachel Hutchinson
40 Waverley Road
Kenilworth
Warwickshire CV8 1JN

Robert Ingham
Parnham House
Beaminster
Dorset DT8 3NA

Ernie Ives
63 Church Lane
Sproughton
Ipswich
Suffolk IP8 3AY

Andy Jackson
See Detail

Roger Jeeves
Saltings
9 Church Road
Hauxton
Cambridgeshire CB2 5HS

Roderick Jenkinson
See Cumberlidge & Jenkinson

Les Jewell
44 Whipton Village Road
Exeter
Devon EX4 8AW

Neil Wyn Jones
2a Groveside
West Kirby
Wirral L48 0QS

Cecil Jordan
c/o Crafts Council
12 Waterloo Place
London SW1Y 4AU

Tobias Kaye
Whites Cross
Lower Dean
Buckfastleigh
Devon TQ11 0LS

Tom Kealy
Boundary Farm
Hare Lane
Buckland St Mary
Chard
Somerset TA20 3JS

Ray Key
The Firs
53 Weston Road
Bretforton
Evesham
Worcestershire WR11 5HW

Mike Kingswood
See Kingswood & Burman

Kingswood & Burman
  Furniture Partnership
The Workshop
Hinton St Mary
Sturminster Newton
Dorset DT10 1NA

Kodoma
203 Avro House
Havelock Terrace
London SW8 4AS

Philip Koomen
Wheelers Barn
Checkendon
Near Reading
Oxfordshire RG8 0NJ

Peter Kuh
2 Recreation Ground
Wingrave
Aylesbury
Buckinghamshire HP22 4PH

Richard La Trobe-Bateman
Elm House
Batcombe
Shepton Mallet
Somerset BA4 6AB

Lasham Furniture Workshop
Manor Farm Buildings
Lasham
Alton
Hampshire GU34 5SL

Ian Laval
Meadowbank Farm
Curthwaite
Wigton
Cumbria CA7 8BG

Lucinda Leech
King Street
Jericho
Oxford OX2 6DF

Patrick Levins
36 Melbourne Street
Livingston
West Lothian EH54 5HW

David Linley Furniture Limited
1 New Kings Road
London SW6 4SB

Peter Lister
Sharpers Barn
Stourton Lodge
Stourton
Shipton on Stour
Warwickshire CV36 5HJ

Trevor Lockie
2 Cnoc Ghlas
Drumbeg
By Lairg
Sutherland IV27 4NW

Nigel Lofthouse
The Old Church
Rishangles
Suffolk IP23 7JZ

Michael Lowe
The Hermitage
Wootton by Woodstock
Oxfordshire OX7 1EQ

John Macfarlan
Lane End Farmhouse,
Longwood
Owslebury
Winchester
Hampshire SO21 1JU

John Mackie
30 Albion Avenue
London N10 1AG

John Makepeace
Parnham House
Beaminster
Dorset DT8 3NA

Bert Marsh
43 Wolverstone Drive
Brighton
Sussex BN1 7FB

Gordon Marsh
Rockholme
Kettlesing
Harrogate
North Yorkshire HG3 2LB

David Marshall
Benar
Penmachno
Betws-y-Coed
Gwynedd LL24 0PS

Guy Martin
4 Moor View
Western Road
Ivybridge
Devon PL21 9AW

Trevor Mayhew
9 Queenswood Avenue
Thornton Heath
Surrey CR4 7HZ

Lucie McCann
37a Fieldhouse Road
London SW12 0HL

Alec McCurdy
Woodland Leaves
Cold Ash
Newbury
Berkshire RG16 9PS

Tony McMullen
1 The Avenue
Blackwell
Bromsgrove
Worcestershire B60 1BW

Henry Mein
Studio M
Main Road
Bleasby
Nottinghamshire NG14 7GH

Martin Midwood
7 The Crescent
Welton
Humberside HU15 1NS

Matthew Morris
Windmill Farm
Biggin Lane
Millington Green
Ashbourne
Derbyshire DE6 3FN

Neville Neal
School House
Stockton
Rugby
Warwickshire CV23 8JE

Nielson & Nielson
2 Dowry Place
Hotwells
Bristol
Avon
BS8 4

Antonios and Ruth Nielson
See Nielson & Nielson

Ian Norbury
White Knight Gallery
28 Painswick Road
Cheltenham
Gloucestershire GL50 2HA

Michael F Norris
Star Brewery Workshops and
Studio
Castle Ditch Lane
Lewes
East Sussex BN7 1YJ

Declan O'Donahue
See S.F. Furniture

Liz and Michael O'Donnell
The Croft
Brough
Thurso
Caithness KW14 8YE

Liam O'Neill
Bay 19
Smithstown
Shannon
County Clare
Ireland

Trevor Oliver
Castle Lodge
3 Castle Hill Gardens
Love Lane
Bodmin
Cornwall PL31 2BH

Garry Olson
17 Stoney Lane
Wilmslow
Cheshire SK9 6LG

Stephen Owen
The Studio
Whipley Manor Farm
Bramley
Surrey GU5 0LL

Jim Partridge
55 Roft Street
Oswestry
Shropshire SY11 2EP

190

Derek Pearce
31 Appach Road
London SW2 2LD

Pearl Dot
2 Roman Way
London N7 8XG

Alan Peters
Aller Studios
Kentisbeare
Cullompton
Devon EX15 2BU

Leslie Plail
4c Lewes Road
Bromley
Kent BR1 2RM

Professional Woodworkers
Limited
1 Church Street
Pewsey
Wiltshire SN9 5DL

David Pye
c/o The Crafts Council
12 Waterloo Place
London SW1Y 4AU

Howard Raybould
32 Monmouth Road
London W2 4UT

Brian Reeves
Coolderry Cottage
Masseys Lane
East Boldre
Beaulieu
Hampshire SO4 27WE

Dave Regester
Millstream Cottage
Higher Town
Sampford Peverall
Tiverton
Devon EX16 7BR

Robert Ridges
Address withheld

John Roberts
22 Schubert Road
Putney
London SW15 2QS

Edward Robinson
51 Oakthorpe Road
Oxford OX2 7BD

Waring Robinson
The Pightle
St Mary's Lane
Hertingfordbury
Hertford SG14 2LF

Christopher Rose
See Pearl Dot

Gordon Russell
See Detail

Desmond Ryan
Doels Farm
Burwash Common
East Sussex TN19 7ND

S.F. Furniture
Acton Turville
Badminton
Avon GL9 1HH

John Sagar
Shutcastle House
Little Drybrook
Coleford
Gloucestershire GL16 8LP

David Savage
21 Westcombe
Bideford
Devon EX39 3JQ

Barnaby Scott
See Waywood

Mike Scott (Chai)
Studio Ten
Warmington Mill
Sandbach
Cheshire CW11 9QW

Rad Segrt
See Waywood

Rupert Senior
See Whitehouse Workshops

Jon Shaw
Street Farm Workshops
Acton Turville
Badminton
Avon GL9 1HH

Silver Lining Workshops
Chester Road
Aldford
Chester CH3 6HJ

Lee Sinclair
Endon House
Laneham
Retford
Nottinghamshire DN22 0NA

Paul Spriggs
The Croft
Silver Street
South Cerney
Cirencester
Gloucestershire GL7 5TR

Philip St Pier
Street Farm Workshops
Acton Turville
Badminton
Avon GL9 1HH

Zyg Staniaszek
See Kodama

Tim Stead
The Steading
Blainslie
Galashiels
Scotland TD1 2PR

Stephenson Brothers
The Workshop
Ashford Road
Bethersden
Ashford
Kent TN26 3AP

Marc and Anthony Stevenson
See Stevenson Brothers

Chris Stott
Croft House
29 High Street
Burringham
Scunthorpe
South Humberside DN17 3NA

Guy Taplin
Anglesea Cottage
Anglesea Road
Wivenhoe
Essex CO7 9JR

Jules Tattersall
Tan Refail
Llanddeusant
Holyhead
Anglesey
Gwynedd LL65 4AD

Ian Taylor
46 Main Street
Lowick
Berwick upon Tweed
Northumberland TD15 2UA

Zachary Taylor
13 Church Field Close
North Harrow
Middlesex HA2 6BD

Malcolm Thomas
Penprompren
Llangwyryfon
Aberystwyth
Dyfed SY23 4EX

Brian Tomnay
58 Polworth Gardens
Edinburgh EH11 1LL

Alan Townsend
3 Green Walk
Marden Ash
Essex CM5 9HR

Trannon Furniture Makers
Llawr-y-Glyn
Caersws
Powys SY17 5RH

Frank Triggs
The Poplars
Gwern-y-Brenin
Oswestry
Shropshire SY10 8AR

John Underhill
5 Wellington Square
Cheltenham
Gloucestershire GL50 4JU

Andrew Varah
Hobley's Furze
Little Walton
Pailton
Rugby
Warwickshire CV23 0GL

Harold Wakefield
20 Rochford Tower Lane
Boston
Lincolnshire PE21 9RG

Rod Wales
Wales & Wales
Longbarn Workshop
Muddles Green
Chiddingly
Lewes
East Sussex BN8 6HW

Robin Wardle
64 Gladstone Street
Fleckney
Leicestershire LE8 0AG

Waywood
Eynsham Park Sawmill
Cuckoo Lane
North Leigh
Witney
Oxfordshire OX8 6PS

David Weldon
14 Brook Road
Epping
Essex CM16 7BT

Ewan Welsh
F1/D Dean Clough Industrial
Park
Dean Clough
Halifax
West Yorkshire HX3 5AX

David West
27 Millgreen
Lyme Regis
Dorset DT7 3PH

Andrew Whateley
c/o 20 Combrook
Warwick CV35 9HP

Charles Wheeler Carmichael
See Whitehouse Workshops

David and Jean Whitaker
Frogge Cottage
Frog Street
Ickleton
Saffron Walden
Essex CB10 1SM

Don White
10 Graham Road
Downend
Bristol
Avon BS16 6AN

Peter White
10 The Russets
Meopham
Kent DA13 0HH

Whitehouse Workshops
Church Street
Betchworth
Surrey RH3 7DN

Peter Wilder
Lydebrook
North Mill
Bledlow
Aylesbury
Buckinghamshire HP17 9QP

Robert Williams
See Pearl Dot Limited

Robin Williams
1 Church Court
Harberton
Totnes
Devon TQ9 7UG

Eric Williamson
Kinetic Sculpture
Tu Hwnt I'rnant
Bont
Dolgadfan
Llanbrynmair
Powys SY19 7AT

Rupert Williamson
5 New Bradwell Workshop
St James Street
New Bradwell
Milton Keynes
Buckinghamshire MK13 0BW

Ferelyth Wills
The Camp
77 Church Road
Steep
Petersfield
Hampshire GU32 2DF

John Wilsher
4c Lewes Road
Bromley
Kent BR1 2RN

Richard Windley
Greystead
Temple Grove
Little Hereford
Ludlow
Shropshire SY8 4LQ

Brian Winter
Milton House
Lyth
Caithness KW1 4UD

Toby Winteringham
42 Goodwins Road
King's Lynn
Norfolk PE30 5QX

Michael Wood
The Cottage
Bosence Meadow
Townshend
Hayle
Cornwall TR27 6AL

Tim and Vicki Wood
Street Farm
Great Fryup Dale
Whitby
North Yorkshire YO21 2AS

Andrew Woodcock
See Chameleon Interior
Furnishing

David Woodward
Studio 6
The Craft Centre
Oxford Road
Hay-on-Wye
Herefordshire HR3 1XX

John Wright
Little Angel Marionette Theatre
14 Dagmar Passage
Cross Street
London N1 2DN

John Wyndham Designs
Muddles Green
Chiddingly
Lewes
East Sussex BN8 6HW